The Open University

A220 Princes and Peoples: France and the British Isles, 1620–1714

Block 3: Parliaments and kings 1660s-1710s

First published in 1995 by

The Open University

Walton Hall

Milton Keynes

United Kingdom

MK7 6AA

ISBN 0 7492 1152 0

Edited, designed and typeset by The Open University.

This book is a component of the Open University course A220 *Princes and Peoples: France and the British Isles, 1620–1714*. Details of this and other Open University courses are available from the Central Enquiry Service, The Open University, PO Box 200, Walton Hall, Milton Keynes, MK7 6YZ, tel.: 01908 653078.

Printed and bound in the United Kingdom by Bell and Bain Ltd, Glasgow

9656C/a220b3pli1.1

Contents

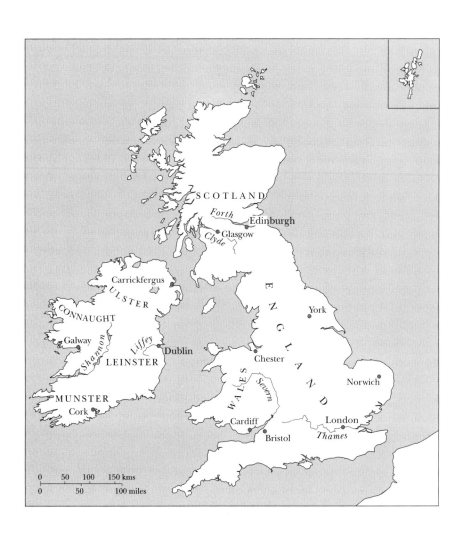

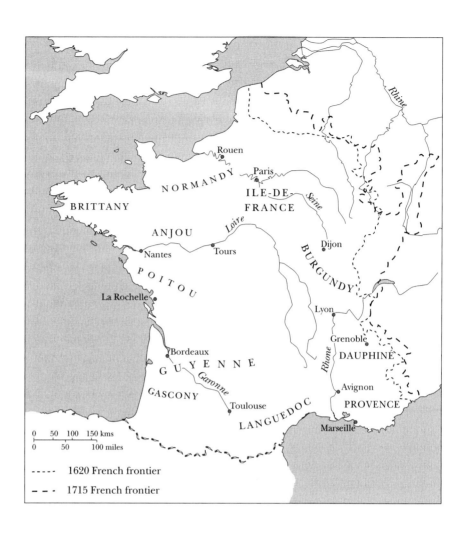

ROUEN

NORMANDY

Paris
ILE-DE-
FRANCE

Seine

BRITTANY

ANJOU

Loire

Dijon

BURGUNDY

Nantes   Tours

POITOU

La Rochelle

Lyon

Grenoble

DAUPHINÉ

Rhône

Bordeaux

GUYENNE

Garonne

GASCONY

Toulouse

Avignon

PROVENCE

LANGUEDOC

Marseille

Rhône

0   50 100 150 kms

0   50   100 miles

- - - - -   1620 French frontier

- - - -   1715 French frontier

Introduction

In the first two blocks we looked at the upheavals in France and the British Isles in the 1640s and 1650s and at the social, religious and administrative changes which took place over the whole of the seventeenth century. In this final block, we shall look at the ways in which both France and England became major powers in Europe, whilst developing very different kinds of government and justifications for those different kinds of government. We shall also look at the ways in which France, as the cultural leader of Europe, made its influence felt in Britain even though for much of the period there was war between the two societies. In the final unit we shall look at the sources we have used and attempt an overview of the period.

There is not as much set reading from Coward and Briggs in this block as there has been in the previous two blocks, but by the end of the block you should have read most of Briggs and Coward. You may find it helpful to look up the relevant sections when you are working through each unit. You will certainly find it helpful when revising the course to go back to them as well as to the units. It is difficult to digest books such as these when you read them straight through, so try setting yourself a question, using the techniques of reading which you practised in earlier units.

Acknowledgements

Apart from the people whose names appear on the written material and on the TV credits many people have worked extremely hard and under difficult circumstances to produce the course. Particular thanks are due to Pat Caldwell, Course Manager, and her predecessors Anne Bullman, Sue Gallagher, and Wendy Simpson, also Lydia Chant; to Anne Howells, editor; to Tony Coulson, liaison librarian; to Professor Colin Jones, external assessor; to Rob Williams and Ray Munns in the studio; and to Janet Fennell, Cheryl O'Toole, Sophie White and Sarah Mowatt of the Electronic Publishing Unit who were constantly asked to type material by the day before yesterday.

Unit 11
Challenges to central government, 1660s to 1714

Prepared for the course team by Arthur Marwick

Contents

Study timetable

Weeks of study	Texts	Video	AC	Set books
2	*Anthology*, III.1–6; Offprints 15, 16, Date Chart			Coward, Briggs

Objectives

By the end of this unit you should:

1 be able to appreciate the contrast between the turbulent political history of the British Isles including 'the Glorious Revolution', and the relatively stable progress of centralized monarchy in France;

2 be in a position to analyse and compare the nature and extent of the political challenges to central government in the different countries and how they were dealt with, and in particular, to discuss knowledgeably the notion that in this period the French monarchy won its struggle with the nobility and the English monarchy lost;

3 be able to assess the character and significance of the different kinds of religious opposition manifested in the different countries;

4 be able to itemize the main outbreaks of popular protest in the various countries, analysing their causes and significance, and identifying the main differences between events in France and events in the British Isles;

5 be able to appreciate the way in which political, religious, and popular protests were often intertwined;

6 have further advanced your skills in historical methodology and in comparative historical study.

Introduction

This unit follows on chronologically from Unit 5, as we resume our study of the upheavals of the mid-seventeenth century and their aftermath. Unit 5 was called 'The return to internal stability' and we saw there how the governments of the different countries restored order to the state. However, you can see from the fact that neither the Frondes nor the civil wars in the British Isles ended neatly and conclusively on a particular date, that there were certain inherent problems which led to continued instability. In the British Isles the monarchy was restored; in France the young Louis XIV was building up the power of central government. In this unit we shall look at the further challenges to central authority and at the reasons for them.

But first we need to understand what general developments took place in religion and politics in the period from the mid-1660s. I shall be asking you to do a good deal of reading from Coward and Briggs, some of which you will come back to in later units, in order that you can get a sense of the changes which took place over the second half of the seventeenth century. There is no video or audio associated with this unit; we have allowed the time for the extra reading.

When you are reading long passages from such books as these it is a good idea to try to make sure that you understand the general trends rather than every single event. Don't let yourself get bogged down making pages of notes or marking every other sentence of the pages of the book. It is much better to read a section at a time, then ask yourself what was being said and make a note of that, looking back to make sure that you have properly understood what was said. Remember to use the date chart in order to get a brief understanding of the chronology. Let us now turn to the challenges to the authority of the state.

Monarchy, government and peoples

Exercise   Read Briggs pp.144–65 and Coward pp.281–365, 395–400 and 428–32 making notes on:

1   what issues led to challenges to the central government (the monarchy in France, the monarch in parliament in England);

2   what popular risings or upheavals took place;

3   what comparisons and contrasts we might draw between the reasons for uprisings or upheavals in France and England.

Discussion   1   My list of issues goes as follows:

France	England
King's arbitrary actions in dealing with Fouquet.	King's requirement for more money.
Taxation (e.g. impositions of 1675 in Bordeaux; increases in indirect taxation).	Lack of toleration for dissenters (Presbyterians, Independents, Baptists, Quakers and Fifth Monarchists).
Further sales of offices.	Pro-Catholic policies of Charles II and James II.
Government borrowing and defaulting on repayments.	Protestant succession.
Debasement of the currency.	
Royal territorial ambitions and continual warfare.	
Compulsory billeting of troops.	
Poverty resulting from agrarian depression.	
Harvest crisis 1693–4; exceptionally severe winter 1708–4; bovine epidemic 1714.	
Religious dissidence (Huguenots and Jansenists).	

2

France	England
1662 Revolt in the Boulonnais.	1661 Venner's Fifth Monarchy rising.
1675 Rising in Brittany.	1678 Popish Plot.
Rising in Bordeaux.	1679–81 Exclusion Crisis.
1702–5 Huguenot rising in the Cévennes.	1683 Rye House Plot.
1707 Rising of Tard-Avisés in Quercy.	1685 Monmouth's rebellion.
	1688 Provincial risings and demonstrations.
	1710 Sacheverell riots.

3   Overwhelmingly the direct challenges to central, that is the king's, authority in France concerned taxation, in particular the level of his exactions during the more or less continuous period of war between 1667 and 1713. But the effects of ever-increasing taxes were exacerbated by food shortages caused by abnormal weather and epidemics.

The contrast with England is very marked. Here, virtually all the serious upheavals were concerned with religious or religio-political issues. The royal requirement for more money was checked by parliament not by popular revolt. The absence of famine and the commercial expansion from the 1660s largely offset the effects of landowners' economic difficulties and of the plague and fire in London in 1665–6. Furthermore, the country as a whole suffered less disruption from war than did France, even though from the accession of William and Mary, England was at war with France for much of the time.

A number of other comparisons and contrasts suggest themselves which I'd like you to bear in mind as you work through the rest of the unit.

1   It is clearly difficult to distinguish between political challenges, religious opposition and popular discontent. For example, there plainly was much popular anti-Catholicism in England and much support for the Protestant succession, but Coward makes the point that Shaftesbury ruthlessly exploited stories of Catholic plots to gain support for the policy of excluding James, Duke of York from the succession (p.332) and that the popular riots at the time of the impeachment of Dr Sacheverell may not have been spontaneous (p.432).

2   In the British Isles (and specifically in England itself) there were small but significant changes in the nature of central government; there were no such changes in France 1669–1715, where, as it were, we are dealing with a 'constant', what, in shorthand, we may refer to as absolute monarchy. There is no call for being jingoistically starry-eyed over the contrasting 'evolution' (as it sometimes used to be expressed) of 'the British Constitution'. Much of what happened was due to contingency; things would surely have been different had James not been a Catholic (or such an open one), had Charles (as many expected) survived him, or had William not been so determined to exploit the English connection in his struggle with Louis. Much more (most historians now argue) was due to the pressures of war. Many of the actual consequences following upon the changes in the succession were not deliberately intended.

3   However (this is so important, and so contentious, I must give it a separate heading), it is also (in my view) the case that in the 1660s English central government was different from that in France: in particular there was in France no equivalent of the English parliament. Although the sentiment of the political nation in England was overwhelmingly monarchist and legitimist (it couldn't just be any old king), parliament could not be dispensed with – the clock, as I put it in Unit 5, could not be completely turned back. But you do not have to agree. Do pay careful heed to Coward's arguments. Note that he declares Danby's failure to control Charles's expenditure 'a major factor in retarding the growth of strong monarchy in England' (p.320), and that his chapter 11 is titled 'The trend towards absolutism'.

4   Challenges to the monarch from within the political nation were far more serious in the British Isles than in France, where, in fact, they were practically non-existent. On the very first page of his survey, Jones (1978) declares that there were three occasions on which civil war might have broken out: 1681 (the Exclusion Crisis); 1685 (Monmouth's Rebellion); 1688 (William's invasion). However, you should read what Coward says as he is more circumspect. But be in no doubt: these were troubled times for the English monarchy.

5   Strong religious commitment continued (like war) to be an inescapable fact of life. Again the dangers to established government were more manifest in England (and Scotland and Ireland). But it is a moot point (try to decide for yourself) whether religious issues

(Jansenism within the Catholic church, Protestantism outside it) were not just as serious a threat in France.

6   To some extent we can, in any case, restore the balance. Popular revolts (linked in turn to much greater poverty and hardship) were much more prevalent and dangerous in France.

7   Both Scotland and Ireland, though in rather different ways, posed problems for the English government. Both, though especially Ireland, could be the launching pads for foreign invasion. Ireland, whether with or without its own parliament, was ruled by England; a majority of the population was disaffected from that rule – and thus of course government in Dublin could itself at times fall under threat. Scotland (till 1707) was a separate state, traditional enemy of England. The fact of the union of the crowns could mean that specifically Scottish tensions could spill over into England, while also, of course, menacing Scottish government in Edinburgh. Religious conflicts were particularly strong in both Ireland and Scotland. Dearth, always a potential breeder of popular protest, was rampant in both Ireland and the Scottish Highlands.

8   For many of the issues we are studying, the primary sources are lacking, or unclear and ambiguous. One might well want to ask whether the growth of party (Whigs and Tories) strengthened or weakened central government: Coward tells us that because of the inadequacies of the source material it is hard to be sure how far there really was a growth of party. When it comes to popular movements sources are inevitably scarce and sometimes their authenticity is in doubt. Sometimes visual sources and physical artefacts (e.g. playing cards, pub signs) are useful, but have to be interpreted with even more than the usual caution.

Let us now look in detail at some of the challenges to royal authority.

Challenges in France, 1669–1714

Ruler of the widespread, diverse territories that made up France, Louis XIV, despite his effective centralized administration, depended on his nobles. His nobles, for the most part, were not interested in participating in central government as long as they could share in the spoils (i.e. taxation) of regional government. To say that Louis crushed the French nobility would be incorrect. He tamed them and exploited them, setting them, of course, within the efficient web of influence created by Colbert. The princely nobles who had opposed the monarchy in the Frondes had in any case lost popularity in their own regions, and Louis took special care to neutralize them. The Prince de Condé was appointed governor of Languedoc, the Prince de Conti of Burgundy. But these appointments were for three years at a time; and there were always the eagle eyes of the *intendants*, often noble also, but appointed by the king from a different part of France. For the potentially dangerous duc de la Rochefoucauld,

Louis in 1669 created the new high office of Grand Master of the Wardrobe – powerless, but under Louis's nose: as Mettam (1988, p.93) puts it, 'Louis could keep a close watch on him, and the duke could hope that, if he gave devoted service, it might one day bring his family the recognition as princes in their own right which he so much desired'. As we have seen Languedoc had been a trouble-spot, but now the indigenous nobles were happy to enter into a stable partnership with the crown, their docility being rewarded with a greater share of the profits of the tax system (Beik, 1988, pp.245–328). One impressive type of evidence (apart from the absence of risings involving the nobles) of the systematic power of the central government is the way in which the correspondence between the centre and the provinces becomes more organized and orderly in the period 1661–1715. The three official letters from Colbert (*Anthology*, III.1) are more transparent than most primary sources usually are, and indicate clearly Colbert's methods of maintaining control (though, of course, they do not tell us what results he obtained).

Exercise   Read *Anthology*, III.1 (A)–(C) making notes on the following questions.

1   In what ways, in his letter to the *intendant* at Caen, does Colbert indicate his control over (a) the *intendant* (there is unwitting as well as witting testimony), and (b) the minor official? Why is the message to this official to be kept private? Any comments on Colbert's cunning here?

2   Discuss as fully as you can how Colbert is trying to control the important noble, the duc de Chaulnes, and how this fits into royal policy.

3   Explain 'memoirs' and '*élections*' in the letter to the *intendant* at Paris. How in this letter is Colbert demonstrating how he controls the *intendants*?

Discussion   1   Unwittingly it is revealed that Colbert requires detailed letters from his *intendants*; wittingly that he is prepared to go over the *intendant*'s head to reprimand and cancel the action of a minor official. The punishment threatened for any similar piece of initiative is fearsome. But Colbert is too cunning to permit this threat to give people the excuse for not paying their taxes that the collector himself is out of favour; that is why the message is to be private.

2   Colbert is warning the duke that if he can't get the provincial estates to deliver approval for the new levies that will be taken as showing that he does not have the respect of his own province, while if he does succeed that will bring him greater glory with the king. There is then the veiled threat that an *intendant* might have to be appointed for Brittany. The final threat is that failure will be taken as showing ill will against the king, and that de Chaulnes will be regarded as personally responsible for this. This carrot-and-stick approach very much fits into the royal policy of taming and exploiting the nobles.

3   'Memoirs' are 'notes' or 'records', '*élections*' are 'districts'. This letter is to one *intendant* but we can deduce that it is a fair sample of
Colbert's methods with all *intendants*. He sends out detailed instructions and expects immediate and frequent replies. He will not
accept superficial and hasty work: above all, *intendants* must do the
investigating directly themselves and must not rely on local officials.
The constant reference, of course, is to satisfying the king.

Challenges in England

The Exclusion Crisis, 1679–81

For this episode, one of those, according to Jones (1978), fraught with
the possibility of civil war, we shall rely on the detailed account given in
Coward, together with *Anthology*, III.2. I want you to re-read Coward from
the beginning of the last paragraph on p.324 to the end of the second
paragraph on p.334. Then I want you to read through the clauses of the
1680 Exclusion Bill (*Anthology*, III.2).

Exercise   As a comprehensive political history Coward's book does not focus
specifically on the issues we are concerned with, so you will find it helpful
if you focus on these questions, graded in ascending order of seriousness:

1   How strong was opposition to the court, and how serious was the
general political turbulence and stability?

2   How close was a significant diminution in the royal prerogative?

3   How near was civil war?

4   How was it that for all the opposition and turbulence the monarchy
survived unscathed?

Discussion   As clear answers are offered by Coward I am not going to set out any of
my own. However, with respect to question 4, above, I would like to be
sure that you noted the following points:

(a)   Political turbulence did not all tend in the one direction (there was
a Tory reaction in favour of the monarchy; while the alleged Popish
Plot – at first – discredited the monarchy, the alleged Rye House
Plot discredited the Whigs).

(b)   Charles's newly found 'financial strength which allowed him in 1681
to dispense with parliament'.

(c)   Charles's astuteness in 'strategically timed concessions'.

(d)   'The monarchy was much stronger than in 1641–2. Scotland and
Ireland were subservient.'

(e)   The Whigs were not as strong as they appeared, and 'were no more willing than the Tory magnates to plunge the country into another rebellion and civil war'. (These last four points are from Coward, pp.331–2.)

Now, with regard to the 1680 Exclusion Bill: the phrasing is very ominous. Not only is the (completely legitimate) heir to the throne pronounced 'excluded and made for ever incapable to inherit', again and again it is repeated that anyone aiding or supporting his claim is guilty of high treason. But as you now know very well, you do not take the words of a document in isolation: you must bring in its origins and full context. The Bill represents the view of the Whigs, more particularly of Shaftesbury, who, shortly after, was sent into exile. Clearly the Bill represented an enormous potential threat to the monarchy; but the crucial fact is that it was never enacted.

Monmouth and the Western Rising, 1685

One of the problems faced by the Whigs was finding a suitable alternative heir to James, Duke of York (they had no wish for a return to republican government). Coward explains (pp.330–1) why the choice fell on James, Duke of Monmouth, some of whose supporters, indeed, put around the story that he was actually legitimate, Charles having allegedly gone through a secret marriage with Monmouth's mother, Lucy Walter. From being a callous rowdy in his youth, Monmouth, some historians assert (not Coward), had become a distinguished soldier (and even, perhaps, minor statesman). At the instigation of Shaftesbury, and in defiance of the king, Monmouth in 1680 had gone on a princely progress through the West Country.

> Outside each town a procession of gentry on horseback and commoners on foot set out, up to several hundred in number, to march with him to his host's residence. At Bath two hundred townsmen and country folk braved the bishop's displeasure, escorting Monmouth into the town to the accompaniment of bells and bonfires; while at Exeter the church was defied once again, several hundred youths dressed in white leading their guest to the city centre, crying out 'God Bless the Protestant Duke'... Pamphlets were distributed in town and village, as the procession swept by, claiming that the duke's legitimacy would be proven by people 'yet alive'; and perhaps carried away by the moment's intoxication Monmouth touched once – at Crewkerne – for the King's Evil.
>
> ... though his Protestant religion and Whig allies doubtless accounted for some of the cheering, Monmouth could be in no doubt that he was the principal centre of attention. His entrances into towns were impressive: at the age of thirty he was still youthful and handsome, a tall figure on horseback, the mounted escort proclaiming his military reputation, the deferential train of followers, his royal birth. (Clifton, 1984, pp.127–8)

Monmouth was in exile in Brussels when his father died unexpectedly in February 1685, to be succeeded unopposed by James. The scene was being set for the second of the possible civil wars identified by Jones (1978). While Charles was alive Monmouth could always hope for restoration to royal favour; now it was either permanent exile, or immediate action. He could, we have seen, count on much popular support; he was himself a proven soldier and leader of men; as former captain-general of the army he could hope that the regular forces would not actually oppose him. They would in any case be divided if the Earl of Argyll could land in Scotland while he landed in the West Country. The weather (like beauty) is a neglected force in history; Argyll got off to Scotland in May, while Monmouth remained holed up in port, finally landing at Lyme Regis on

Figure 1
Contemporary playing cards illustrating Monmouth's rebellion 1685 – Queen of Diamonds ('the godly Maids of Taunton presenting their Colours upon their knees to ye D. of M.'), Knave of Clubs ('Ferguson preaching to the Rebells ye day before ye defeat on Iosh.22.v.22'), King of Spades ('Devills in ye Ayre Bewitching M's army'), Three of Spades ('The Late Duke of M: taken near the Ld Grey').

11 June. This failed co-ordination was almost cancelled out by the blunders of the government, who expected Argyll to land in Northern Ireland (note this constant strategic worry about Ireland), and Monmouth in the north of England. However, the more profound forces were against Monmouth. Parliament, with the new succession, was newly elected, and loyal to James. James got the cash he needed; Monmouth had little. Most of the nobility and gentry had little taste for further turmoil, and less sympathy for the popular elements supporting Monmouth.

Monmouth remained three days at Lyme Regis, where he issued his first Proclamation; volunteers poured in at an encouraging rate. As he marched triumphantly to Taunton the local militia melted away. Ecstatically received in Taunton, Monmouth issued his second (revised) Proclamation (*Anthology*, III.3).

Exercise   If you now read this Proclamation (*Anthology*, III.3) carefully you should be able to spot the (relatively modest) claim made in the first Proclamation, as well as noting the much firmer claim being made in this one.

1   What was his first claim?

2   Why, do you think (this is not spelt out in the document – you need to bring your wider knowledge to bear), was that particular formulation a further obstacle to winning the support of the nobility and gentry?

3   What reasons does Monmouth himself give for changing his claim?

Discussion   1   The decision to declare him king would be left to 'a parliament legally chosen and acting with freedom'. Note that he accepts parliament's role as kingmaker.

2   The nobility and gentry wanted certainty, and they supported legitimacy – James was the legitimate king, even Monmouth was still only calling himself duke. What they did not want was all the turmoil and uncertainty of a new parliament being elected, and then the vital decision being left to that parliament; decision by parliament, in any case, being in conflict with the principle of succession entirely by hereditary right (Monmouth knew he had made a mistake, but of course he couldn't say so openly – note again how carefully you must read historical sources). Consider, too, the effect on the noble families of England of admitting that an illegitimate child might have a legitimate claim to succeed his father.

3   The major substantive reason Monmouth gives is that, being proclaimed king, he will immediately have sovereign authority and be able to make use of the laws and statutes of the realm. This in turn, he says, will speed his progress and mean less damage to the kingdom and people. Above all, in insisting upon his own reluctance to make the change, he stresses that he was acting on the advice, and in the interests, of 'our own people'.

Bridgwater was occupied. The plan for attacking Bristol from the east was an imaginative one and if carried out promptly might (a) have succeeded and (b) brought a transformation in the military situation. But ... rain stopped play. By the time Monmouth was able to ignite his guns, the able Colonel Oglethorpe (whose regulars showed no compunction about opposing Monmouth) had rumbled the planned surprise attack (Clifton, 1984, pp.182–3). Monmouth had to withdraw south westwards. Again there was the possibility of a surprise attack on government forces gathered on Sedgmoor, when an accidental pistol shot gave the game away. Beginning as a chapter of accidents, Sedgmoor turned into a massacre.

Monmouth was captured three days after the battle, hiding in a ditch. He was executed as a traitor. Coward (p.337) gives an efficient summary of the social composition of his followers and of the fundamental reasons for the failure of this challenge to central government. As in France, the government's ultimate weapon against the recurrence of such rebellion was terror. Hundreds were flogged at the cart tail, seventy-year-old Dame Alice Lisle was sentenced to burning, commuted to beheading, about 250 were choked half unconscious, disembowelled, then pickled in brine and coated in tar, put on display as a public warning, many died in prison, hundreds were transported (saving the costs of execution and bringing a small profit to the government). Coward is probably right that the propertied classes did not much care about the round of punishments carried out soon after Sedgmoor; but it may be that the delayed second round, instituted at the end of September, did cause, as popular legend has always had it, a certain revulsion against James.

The Glorious Revolution, 1688

The account in Coward is clear: re-read pp.334–44, keeping the following points in mind:

1   The management of parliament, amounting almost to 'packing' was the product not just of James's activities, but was a policy initiated by Charles II. It may indicate a movement towards absolutism; it certainly indicates that parliament itself could not be ignored (a problem Louis XIV was free of).

2   The central phenomenon would appear to be James's 'collapse of nerve' (p.344). Remarking that James had a standing army of perhaps 40,000, to William's invading army of around 14,000, and that James panicked over the desertion to William of a mere 1,000 of his men, Speck (1989) declares, 'Thus in the event the Revolution hinged on the personality and mental state of James II'. It seems extraordinary that with such a loyal parliament, James should so quickly have antagonized them. Revolutions, we might well reflect, may have profound consequences, but that does not necessarily mean they have profound causes.

3   The attitude of nobility and gentry, however, is important: hostile to Monmouth, it was, in 1688, perhaps neutral rather than supportive of James; and note the positive support for William of Delamere, Devonshire and Danby.

4   The term 'glorious' was used first to apply to William's undertaking of November 1688; the term 'Glorious Revolution' was first used in the autumn of 1689, 'glorious' essentially implying 'bloodless'.

However, events were far from bloodless in Ireland, to which we must now turn.

Ireland

Under Charles II, we noted from Coward, Ireland had been subservient. Turn now to Offprint 15, which is part of a chapter from the principal general history of Ireland in the early modern period, *A New History of Ireland*, volume 3.

Figure 2
Contemporary playing card of c.1690 – Knave of Hearts depicting 'Tyrconnel arming ye Papists in Ireland'. British Museum Dept of Prints and Drawings 1896-5-1-919, reproduced by permission of the Trustees of the British Museum.

Exercise   Read the essay carefully, making notes on the main developments (you may also want to look at your date chart), and answer the following questions:

1 (a) The first three pages of this extract indicate the author's very strong commitment to history as a systematic discipline. How?

(b) Is it possible to write unbiased history of events such as 'the war of the two kings'?

(c) With reference to that question, how would you describe this piece of history by J.G. Simms?

2   What elements indicate that this war is a European matter, not purely English and Irish?

3   Which more concerned James: (a) the English crown and its powers; or (b) the cause of Catholics in Ireland? Explain your answer.

4   James, remember, though now displaced by William, had been legitimate king. Is it reasonable, therefore, to argue that if he, not William, had won 'the war of the two kings', this would have involved a blow to the stability of the English monarchy? (This is a tough question, though your responses to Q.3 should help. Spend a bit of time on it, and jot down major points even if you can't develop a complete paragraph.)

Discussion   1 (a) The main point is that these paragraphs offer a critical analysis of the primary sources for this study (and also of one secondary source, by the nineteenth-century historian, Macaulay). You may have noticed, too, Simms's belief that the events of the seventeenth century were to have a great impact on Ireland's later history (Offprint 15, pp.83, 84, 87).

(b) Simms indicates that Macaulay was strongly 'Williamite' and that English historians have generally followed in this tradition. Among the general public, there are strongly held views on both sides, which emphasize the obligation of the professional historian to analyse all the sources rigorously to strive for an unbiased history.

(c) It seems to me that, indeed, Simms succeeds marvellously in writing an unbiased history.

2   William was fighting on two fronts. James had French support. The international character of William's army. Battle of Boyne acclaimed in Europe (including Catholic Austria) as victory over France. Ginkel (William's Commander-in-Chief) saw Ireland as a side-show to war in the Netherlands.

3   (a) The English crown. He would not permit the repeal of Poyning's law (which gave the king's council in England powers over the Irish parliament). He was reluctant to allow the implementation of any measures which would have taken lands from Protestant planters and restore them to Catholics. He did not re-establish the Catholic church.

4   Even the Catholic parliament (essentially made up of Old English) contemplated self-government under the English crown. And James clearly wanted to be a king with wide support (summoning Church of Ireland bishops; releasing the 10,000) On the other hand:

(a) Even if he did win in Ireland, he would still have had to conquer England.

(b) If he did regain the English crown, it would be subject to strong French influence.

(c) William had by no means unanimous support, but James by this time would be significantly more divisive as a king.

(d) James had been lawful king; his restoration could be seen as a triumph for monarchy. But William was now the man in possession; his overthrow would be a defeat for central government as it had now evolved.

There one might leave Ireland. However Connolly (1992, pp.233–7) argues that Irish disaffection and discontent continued to be a serious threat to the stability of the English monarchy until at least 1720.

Scotland

In his Introduction to Part 5, which you have already read, Coward characterizes the period 1689–1714 as one of 'extreme political instability'. The impression I derive from what follows (pp.351–445) is that this 'instability' is focused on parliament, which, under the pressures of war, is becoming increasingly important, and that the monarchy is insulated from it. Note, however, that Coward raises the issue, at the very end of our period of 'A Jacobite Restoration or Hanoverian succession?' (p.440), speaking on the next page of 'the country teetering on the edge of civil war'. Consider this very carefully. Otherwise the main threats to monarchical central government seem to come:

- from relations with Scotland and questions of the succession;

- from religious conflict and popular disturbances.

Now read Coward, pp.351–445, noting down how far your understanding of these pages coincides with the summary I have just given. Then turn to Coward pp.413–22 and note down what challenges to royal authority might come from Scotland. We shall return to these subjects later in the unit.

With James's flight William became king of England; was he also, thereby, king of Scotland? The Convention Parliament which met in Edinburgh in March 1689 was not in any way committed to supporting William. However, James had lost his hold on the mechanisms of controlling the Scottish parliament (notice again how important parliament is in this sense, even in Scotland); the letter he sent to Edinburgh (he was at that moment leading his troops in Ireland) was offensively autocratic, that of William conciliatory. On 4 April the Scottish parliament resolved

with only five dissentients that James had forfeited the crown, and on 11
April adopted the Claim of Right which settled the succession on William
and Mary and their heirs. John Graham of Claverhouse, Viscount Dundee, did, at Dundee Law in April 1689, raise the standard for James. He
was victorious at the Battle of Killiecrankie, but was himself killed. Led by
Colonel Alexander Cannon, the triumphant Jacobite army moved south,
only to meet decisive defeat at Dunkeld by a regiment of Cameronians.

As I pointed out in Unit 5, turbulence and faction in the Highlands
were always a threat to central authority. The Highland chieftains,
accordingly, were called upon to take an oath of allegiance to William by
1 January 1692. The massacre of the MacDonalds of Glencoe on 13
February by royal regiments manned by their hereditary enemies, the
Campbells, because of their failure to meet this deadline, has become
one of the most notorious of the tragic tales with which Scottish history is
littered. It has taken a scholarly work by Paul Hopkins, to restore a sense
of perspective: the MacDonalds delayed as long as they did in the hope of
a French invasion on behalf of James (Hopkins, 1986, p.491). The
government believed that it must crush any threat of a further Jacobite
rising (it also believed, it must be admitted, that brutal Highlanders mer-
ited the most brutal treatment).

There were much more widespread and potent causes of friction
between Scotland and England, as we have seen in Coward, pp.415–19.

Exercise   Turn to *Anthology*, III.4.

1   Identify the key passage in this document, by quoting the exact
       wordings and giving the paragraph and line reference (note that
       some of the words Coward uses are not the exact words of the Act).

2   What is the significance of this passage (a) for the security of
       English central government and (b) for the development of Anglo-
       Scottish relations? (no need to guess; it's all in Coward).

Discussion   1   3rd para., beginning line 9: 'providing always that the same be not
       successor to the crown of England, unless ...'

2   (a) The Scots are threatening to choose a monarch different from
       whoever succeeds in England; Scotland under a separate monarchy
       would at once be a serious threat to England. (b) The situation was
       now so serious that there appeared to be only two courses: complete
       separation or union. The English opted for union, and so did a suf-
       ficient number of influential Scots.

Those Scots would have preferred a federal (i.e. preserving a local Scottish parliament), rather than an incorporating union. According to Lenman (1980, p.80) the English gained their way in three stages:

1   Blackmail (principally through the Aliens Act – see Coward) of the
       Scottish nobles, who in turn dominated the lairds and burgesses.

2   A snap vote in an empty Scottish parliament delegated the central issues to four Scottish Commissioners to be chosen by Queen Anne.

3   Certain provisions in the Treaty (particularly the economic ones) were in effect bribes for the Scottish nobles.

In a nutshell: the English were skilful; enough influential Scots felt their own economic interests would be well served by incorporating Union. Lenman points out that these supporters of Union were careful not to allow elections to the new Union parliament; the first Scottish MPs there were in fact chosen directly by the now-to-be-abolished Scottish parliament. This, says Lenman, indicates the fear of 'an anti-Union landslide in an early election'. 'The Jacobites certainly regarded the Union as a major policy gift to them, for it handed them the leadership of nationalist sentiment in Scotland' (Lenman, 1980, p.87).

There was, in March 1708, an attempted invasion by 'James III' (son of James II, who had died in 1702). Ships with 5,000 soldiers on board stood off Crail and Pittenweem on the Fife coast of the Firth of Forth. Forty miles away Jacobite lairds in Stirlingshire tried to raise the countryside but were crippled by the absence of support from any great noble (this is a consistent theme). Lacking support in the immediate vicinity James did not attempt landings, and his fleet was chased by Admiral Byng, all round Britain and back to Dunkirk. In November five lairds were tried for high treason, but, for lack of witnesses, the case was adjudged 'not proven'.

The role of religion

In the previous section the religious dimension to political challenge was very apparent. In the preface to the collection which they edited, Harris, Seaward and Goldie (1990) speak of 'a generation of people locked into a religious cold war'. Coward writes (p.325): 'There was no Popish Plot', and, like many other historians, explains the violence against Catholics as 'hysteria and panic' (p.327). Scott (1990, p.109) rejects the notion of hysteria: 'these events are characterized by a pitiless determination and a cold-blooded cruelty which is the opposite of hysterical: it is systematic'. Perhaps we should agree that the reactions to the alleged plot were *both* hysterical *and* systematically cruel. Scott continues: 'It was concerns about religion, not about politics or economics, which drove seventeenth-century English people to compromise their political allegiances and mire themselves in one another's blood'. Then he makes the point which I want to take as my key for this section: 'the experience of England in this respect was anything but unique, and it cannot be explained within a national framework. The religious division concerned was not English, but European' (p.110).

In France, actually, the sources of conflict were both between Catholics and Protestants and within the Catholic church (Briggs, pp.183–92, tells you all you need to know about the Jansenist quarrel, though note that a new purge of the Jansenists began after 1703); and in the British Isles they were both between Catholics and Protestants and between Anglicans and Dissenters.

Louis's ultramontane policy, the policy of trying to establish a French Catholic church free of papal interference, culminated in the Four Articles of 1682. Policies towards the Huguenots were erratic. There were attempts to accommodate Protestant beliefs, but these had little chance since the French Catholic hierarchy could not agree upon one unified policy towards Protestantism. In any case, from 1676 Louis followed an intensified strategy of trying to secure Protestant conversions.

Figure 3
Violent persecution of Protestants at Niort, January 1684, engraving. Bibliothèque des Arts Décoratifs, Paris. Photo: Jean-Loup Charmet.

Early in 1685 certain Huguenots were negotiating with the Earl of Argyll and William of Orange (remember Scott's point about the international context). On 22 October Louis issued the Declaration of Fontainebleau. This revoked the toleration guaranteed by the Edict of Nantes, called for the destruction of Protestant churches, banishment of ministers, and cessation of all Protestant services. All of these were enforced by the notorious *dragonnades*, officially just the billeting of soldiers on the civilian population, in fact murderous attacks by companies of dragoons (news of which soon spread to Britain, further inflaming anti-Catholic sentiment).

The Declaration was popular with most ordinary Catholics in France, but it was regarded sceptically by the pope, and it divided the hierarchy. Conversions increased, but 'new converts' could be a sullen and unpredictable element within the community. People suspected of continuing to be Protestants were sent to *hôpitaux généraux* (see Unit 9), those who refused to compromise went underground or emigrated, many to England and Ireland where their skills as clothworkers were much valued. The leading authority has argued that in some respects Protestants gained from the Declaration (insofar as it 'divided' powerful Catholics, and created a dangerous Protestant 'underground'); Louis certainly gained nothing (Orcibal, 1951 pp.94–165).

Religious repression, famine conditions, and the exactions of government, as expressed through the zealously severe Basville, appointed *intendant* for Languedoc in 1685, produced in the isolated, mountainous, Cévennes region of Languedoc, the series of violent disturbances known as the War of the Camisards, and lasting eight years from 1702. The Camisards had many of the characteristics of religious fanaticism. However, Ducasse (1978, pp.288, 235) has declared that there was a 'majestic gravity' in their religious faith: he quotes the cry of their ablest leader, Pierre Laporte, known as Rolland, 'general of the Children of God': 'Long live the Sword of the Eternal! Liberty of Conscience or Death'. The Camisards tied up 60,000 desperately needed soldiers. In the end, after the most appalling atrocities (not confined to one side), Louis had failed to suppress Protestantism.

In the British Isles the nearest equivalent (in an earlier period) of the Camisards are the extreme Covenanters, known as the Cameronians. These were Presbyterians who refused to accept the restitution of bishops to the Church of Scotland at the Restoration. In the aftermath of the decisive defeat at Bothwell Bridge (1679), and despite the moderation of Monmouth, Cameron and twenty followers issued their Declaration of 22 June 1680: Charles II was 'a tyrant and usurper' and his supporters 'enemies of our Lord Jesus Christ'. The excesses of the Cameronians provided the pretext for the persecution of moderate Covenanters, leading into the 'Killing Time', which lasted from 1684 till the toleration proclaimed by James II in 1687. All in all about hundred executions were carried out, many were killed in the field, many more transported, mutilated, or confined under starvation conditions in plague-ridden make-shift gaols. In his very dispassionate account, Cowan (1976, pp.123, 133) concludes that government policy was designed to harry all dissent into conformity.

That's not all I have to say on religion: it reappears in major popular rioting right at the end of our period.

Popular protest

The era of periodic subsistence crises began to draw to a close in England towards the end of the seventeenth century; the number of local crises in France was also becoming smaller, but in the two years 1693 and 1694 the dearth across France was so devastating that Lachiver (1991) has compared the loss of life to that of the First World War; there was again famine in 1709. Distress, and the violence so often associated with it, was endemic in Ireland and parts of Scotland, but in England there were no serious agrarian disturbances in our period. In France there were three distinct outbreaks of grain rioting: in 1678 at St Tropez and April 1679 at Marseille and Arles; in 1692, four riots in different parts of France; and in January to May 1709 about a dozen outbreaks (with, of course, isolated instances throughout the period). Mobs of up to a couple of thousand could be involved, with women often prominent (Pillorget, 1975, pp.963–75). However the two truly serious popular risings, in Brittany in 1675 and Quercy in 1707 were both provoked by new taxes on legal documents (always important to peasants concerned about rights to land) and largely directed against the tax collectors, though the Breton Revolt was quite complex.

Figure 4
Ruined peasants become wandering beggars, engraving. Bibliothèque Nationale de France, Cabinet des Estampes, Paris.

If you turn now to *Anthology*, III.5, you will see how extensive were the demands of the Torrében rebels, and get some invaluable insights into peasant life: labour services are to be abolished (4); wine taxes are to be controlled (7); tobacco is to be provided at mass (8); fees for priests and lawyers are to be limited (9&10); hunting (pastime of nobles, destructive of crops) is to be abolished in the growing season; millers are to give fair measure. (You should note that there are minor variations, and a few illegible words in the only two copies of this wonderful document which have survived; at one time some historians had doubts about its authenticity – but experts have since cleared these up – see Garlan and Nieves (1975, p.101).)

Exercise   Having read *Anthology*, III.5, I now want you to answer the following questions.

1   Where does the Code refer to the original cause of the riots?

2   How revolutionary is clause 5?

3   What does clause 6 reveal about peasant attitudes and beliefs?

Discussion   1   The second part of 10, stating that the stamp duty is to be abolished (in colourful and symbolic style).

2   Authorities differ here. Garlan and Nieves argue that in *ancien régime* France to suggest intermarriage between peasants and nobility was tantamount to treason. However, the internationally known historian, Roland Mousnier (1971, p. 136) does not find this demand odd.

3   To the peasants the hated salt tax is a human being, an evil woman.

The governor was almost powerless, but with harvest time, the peasants returned to their fields. To mollify the towns, the provincial estates were recalled. They agreed the 'normal' levy, and in return the stamp duty was withdrawn. All very revealing of the balance of power in 'absolutist' France; Louis couldn't always get everything he wanted, but in the end he usually got most of it.

For the Quercy rising of 1707 I want you to turn to Offprint 16. Take careful notes for your own purposes, then do the following exercise.

Exercise   1   Sources for humble people are always scarce. What sources does Bercé use?

2   Does he present the Tard-Avisés as noble fighters on behalf of a unified oppressed class?

Discussion   1   Letters from the *intendant*, Legendre, to the central government; proceedings of the trials of the Tard-Avisés.

2   Very much not. They are looters, often drunk, and they terrorize their neighbours into joining them. They are actively opposed by the ordinary townsfolk.

Nothing to worry about here; no need to make value judgements. Obviously the lack of unity in such a rising, though it did seem quite dangerous for a time, limited the risk to the central government.

Urban riots in Britain were more dangerous, because they were often articulated to the major political and religious issues of the day. During the protracted Exclusion Crisis, Whig demonstrations, organized 'pope-burning processions', etc., kept up the tension. Had all the popular support gone to the Whigs that could have been very serious indeed, but,

Figure 5
The famine of 1693 – the rich
are politely served, the poor
are bludgeoned into a queue,
engraving. Bibliothèque
Nationale de France, Cabinet
des Estampes, Paris.

in fact, the popular classes were just as divided as their noble superiors. Tory crowds were a counter-force to be reckoned with. And it is in fact with Tory rioting that I end this unit.

At the end of February 1710, the Anglican cleric, Dr Henry Sacheverell was put on trial in Westminster Hall by the Whig Government. To see what he was accused of turn now to *Anthology*, III.6 and compare the account with that given by Coward from p.429 to the end of the first paragraph on p.431.

Coward is concerned, very properly, to emphasize the mistakes made by the Whigs, but what I want you to concentrate on here is the systematic and organized nature of the rioting mobs. Drawing upon the leading authority, Professor Geoffrey Holmes, Coward does in fact give a most effective summary in the last of the paragraphs I have just asked you to read. Holmes has also brought out how, while the 'mobs' (many of whose members were respectable professional or trades people) played their part, Anglican ministers used their pulpits systematically in the support of Sacheverell and his cause.

Very clearly the Whigs lost from the Sacheverell episode. That is not the same, however, as saying that the security of central government itself was threatened, except insofar as the Whigs were the strongest and most unequivocal supporters of the succession as then legally established. What is true is that party politics, closely integrated with urban populations which took a passionate interest in the national issues of the day, were a powerful source of a type of instability not to be found in France, where protest were more often over what were seen as violations of local rights.

Conclusion

Let us now return to the points which I set out on pp.5–6. Looking at points 1 and 5 you can see how, especially in England, Scotland and Ireland, religious issues were an integral part of the Glorious Revolution in England, the Williamite war in Ireland and the Jacobite cause in Scotland. They were also important in the popular protests of the Cévennes and in the Exclusion Crisis, the Sacheverell affair and the covenanting campaigns in Scotland.

But also you can see that religion was not just another name for politics. Confessional differences mattered because people *believed.* Catholics in Ireland and Scotland, anti-episcopalian Covenanters in Scotland, Nonconformists in England, Jansenists and Huguenots in France were prepared to go to great length in defence of their beliefs. On the other side there were those members of the church hierarchy who were not prepared to accept changes in the established church (as the Church of Scotland supporters of episcopacy) or in the relations between the established church and the monarchy (as non-juring bishops in 1688).

In points 2, 3 and 4, I referred to changes in the central government of the British Isles and particularly to those in England and to the role of parliament in England (after 1707 in England and Scotland). Perhaps the greatest contrast between challenges to royal authority in France and the British Isles in the second half of the seventeenth century is that in France these came largely from outside the political nation, while in the British Isles it was the political nation and especially parliament which led the opposition. The French rebels were largely the poor and the Protestants, outsiders who felt intolerably oppressed, though they might make reference to ancient rights and liberties. In the British Isles opposition to royal authority came from those who wanted to defend the interests and 'liberties' of other institutions in the state: the church, the Protestant succession (or in the case of Jacobites the hereditary succession), and parliament. The challenges of the political nation were strong enough to ensure James II's deposition in England but to mean that William III had a serious task in suppressing Jacobite support in Ireland and Scotland.

Real material hardship seems to have lain behind many of the revolts in France. In England neither the levels of taxation (which was, in any case, the subject of much parliamentary dispute) nor the impact of natural disasters was acute enough to lead to popular uprisings in England. In Scotland and Ireland, which continued to be subject to famine after it had ceased to have a major impact in England, levels of taxation remained low.

Finally, note how difficult it is really to distinguish between religious and political uprisings, economic and popular disturbances. In almost all the instances we've looked at there's a mixture of issues, of causes and of participants. Political, religious and popular protests were often inter-related.

References

Beik, W (1988), *Absolutism and Society in Seventeenth Century France*, Cambridge University Press, Cambridge.

Clifton, R. (1984), *The Last Popular Rebellion: The Western Rising of 1685*, Temple Smith, London.

Connolly, S.J. (1992), *Religion, Law and Power: The Making of Protestant Ireland 1660–1760*, Clarendon Press, Oxford.

Cowan, I. B. (1976), *The Scottish Covenanters 1660–1688*, Gollancz, London.

Ducasse, A. (1978), *La Guerre des Camisards*, Paris.

Garlan, Y. and Nieves, C. (1975), *Les revoltes brettonnes de 1675: papier timbré et bonnets rouges*, Paris.

Harris, T., Seaward, P. and Goldie, M. (eds) (1990), *The Politics of Religion in Restoration England*, Blackwell, Oxford.

Hopkins, P. (1986), *Glencoe and the End of the Highland War*, John Donald, Edinburgh.

Jones, J. R. (1978), *Country and Court: England 1658–1714* , Edward Arnold, London.

Lachiver, M. (1991), *Les Années de Misére*, Fayard, Paris.

Lenman, B. (1980), *The Jacobite Risings in Britain 1689–1746*, Eyre Methuen, London.

Mettam, R. (1988), *Power and Faction in Louis XIV's France*, Macmillan, London.

Moody, T.W., Martin, F.X. and Byrne, F.J. (eds) (1976), *A New History of Ireland*, Vol III, Clarendon Press, Oxford.

Mousnier, R. (1971), *Peasant Uprisings*, George Allen and Unwin, London.

Orcibal, J. (1951), *Louis XIV et les Protestants*, Paris

Pillorget, R. (1975), *Les Mouvements Insurrectionelles de provence entre 156 et 1715*, Paris.

Scott, J. (1990), 'England's troubles: Exhuming the Popish Plot', in Harris et al.

Speck, W.A. (1989), *Reluctant Revolutionaries: Englishmen and the Revolution of 1688*, Oxford University Press, Oxford.

Unit 12
Kings, nobles and ministers and the debate about absolutism

Prepared for the course team by
Bill Purdue

Contents

Study timetable

Weeks of study	Texts	Video	AC	Set books
2	*Anthology*, III.8–13; Offprint 17	Video 11		Coward, Briggs

Objectives

By the end of this unit you should be:

1   aware of the debate about absolutism;

2   aware of the degree to which British and French kings sought absolute power;

3   able to compare the power of the monarchies and the degree of control exerted by central governments in France and the British Isles;

4   able to discuss the view that in the late seventeenth century the constitutional developments of France the British Isles diverged.

1688 and British liberty

An enduring interpretation of British and French constitutional history is that in the late seventeenth century there was a divergence between the constitutional structures of the two states by which France moved towards absolutism and the British towards a limited monarchy.

The decisive moment of divergence, identified so graphically by the great Whig historians of British history, came in 1688 with the Glorious Revolution. The Whig view of 1688 forms a central pillar of the wider Whig interpretation of history. Few historians would now accept the tale of the triumph of good over evil so confidently told by Macaulay, nor many, at least overtly, see 1688 as such a landmark in the benign and systematic development of British institutions by which parliamentary liberties, the rule of law and representative institutions were progressively fortified as did the twentieth-century Whig G. M. Trevelyan. None the less, the Whig view continues to exert an influence not least in the view of 1688 as a decisive watershed with economic and social dimensions linked to its political implications. What follows from it is of considerable importance: the view of eighteenth-century England as more modern, more firmly attached to the nineteenth than the seventeenth century and the converse view of France as doomed to spend a century awaiting an inglorious revolution.

Let us first of all consider the original thesis as put forward in 1849 by one of its most accomplished exponents, Thomas Babington Macaulay.

> The continental revolutions of the eighteenth and nineteenth centuries took place in countries where all traces of the limited monarchies of the middle ages had long been effaced. The right of the prince to make laws and to levy money had during many generations been undisputed. His throne was guarded by a great regular army. His administration could not, without extreme peril, be blamed even in the mildest terms. His subjects held their personal liberty by no other tenure than his pleasure. Not a single institution was left which had within the memory of the oldest man, afforded efficient protection to the subject against the utmost excess of tyranny. Those great councils which had once curbed the regal power had sunk into oblivion. (Macaulay, 1906, pp. 208–9)

Exercise Using the information in the above quotation, try and answer the following questions.

1   How does Macaulay see the power of continental monarchs?

2   What demonstrates the extent of their power?

3   Had they always exercised such power?

Discussion I would expect you to have noted the following.

1   As absolute with a tendency towards tyranny.

2   They make laws, levy taxes and control standing armies.

3   No, once, in the middle ages, the continental monarchies had been limited monarchies but the institutions which had limited their power had been destroyed or made ineffective. He mentions in particular 'those great councils which had once curbed the regal power'.

We may expect that Macaulay thought that something very different had happened in England and indeed he did:

> These calamities our Revolution averted. It was a revolution strictly defensive, and had prescription and legitimacy on its side. Here, and here only, a limited monarchy of the thirteenth century had come down unimpaired to the seventeenth century... That, without the consent of the representatives of the nation, no legislative act could be passed, no tax imposed, no regular soldiery kept up, that no man could be imprisoned, even for a day, by the arbitrary will of the sovereign, that no tool of power could plead the royal command as a justification for violating any right of the humblest subject, were held, both by Whigs and Tories, to be fundamental laws of the realm. (Macaulay, 1906, p.210)

Exercise   Now answer the following questions.

1   Did Macaulay think that the 1688 Revolution introduced new limitations on the power of the king and gave new rights to subjects?

2   How do the limitations on royal power compare with the considerable power of continental monarchs?

Discussion   1   No, the Revolution was conservative in that it protected an ancient constitution.

2   The limitations on royal power listed are the opposite of absolute powers enjoyed by continental monarchs: whereas they could make laws by themselves, tax at will and imprison without trial, English monarchs were limited in their power by parliament and because they were under the law.

We find G. M. Trevelyan taking exactly the same view of 1688 and the common law a century after Macaulay in his *English Social History* (1944), a view he had first proclaimed in his *England under the Stuarts* (1904):

> This great principle, that law is above the executive, was indeed violated during the revolutionary period of the Commonwealth and Protectorate. But it re-emerged at the Restoration, and was confirmed at the Revolution of 1688, which was effected against James II precisely to establish the principle that law was above the King. That mediaeval idea of the supremacy of law as something separate

Figure 6
James II, *painted in exile, c.1690 by unknown artist, oil on canvas, 120.7 cm x 98.4 cm. Courtesy of the National Portrait Gallery, London.*

from and independent of the will of the executive, disappeared in continental countries. But in England it became the palladium of our liberties … (Trevelyan, 1944, p. 247)

This idea of English exceptionalism depends to a great extent upon what it was the exception to, that is continental absolutism. But what was this absolutism, which the British Isles and perhaps Holland so providentially escaped, and of which France is seen as both prototype and archetype? This unit will discuss the utility of the concept of absolutism, the degree to which France in the late seventeenth century became an absolute monarchy and whether we can substantiate the concept of a divergence in the nature of the British and French states.

Absolutism

Some twenty years ago E. H. Kossman was able to write: 'Absolutism still seems an undisputed historical fact, the defining of which has not given rise to substantial difficulties: it was and is considered to be a historical phenomenon connected with the aggrandisement and the centralization of the state and with the increase of its power' (Kossman, 1976, p.3). Recent revisionism has, however, challenged the very existence of absolutism as with Nicholas Henshall (1992, p.210) who considers that the concept, 'perpetuates an early nineteenth-century attempt to label as despotic the absolute monarchies of the early modern period'. Another critic J. Daly (1978, p.250) has, more cynically, suggested that absolutism and absolute monarchy are used to describe regimes, 'where a king has more power than twentieth-century scholars think a seventeenth-century king ought to have had'.

Henshall, you will have noted distinguishes between *absolutism* and *absolute monarchy* and this is an important distinction. As we saw in Unit 1 the term absolutism was not used in the seventeenth century while the term absolute monarchy was. Absolutism tends to be used to describe eighteenth-century as well as seventeenth-century regimes while absolute monarchy, as Roger Mettam (1990, p.45) has written, 'at least has the merit of being found in seventeenth-century political writings'.

Yet Kossman's definition of absolutism leads to the important question as to whether the salient development was the growth of the power of the state rather than the growth of the power of monarchs. 'Can a republic be governed "absolutely" and if so, is such republican absolutism more or less effective than a monarchical one?' is a question he later asks.

Exercise   Can you think of a republican regime in the seventeenth century which can be considered absolutist?

Discussion   Well you could argue that from the 1640s the English parliamentary regime, a republic after 1649, had more power than most monarchs and used it to ride roughshod over the institutions of civil society and over county and urban government, especially during the rule of the major-

Generals 1655–7, but Coward (pp.261–5) suggests that other interpretations are possible.

Kossman (1976, p.13) quotes the statement by the French historian Roland Mousnier that in England, after 1640, parliament exercised, 'an arbitrary, absolute and truly sovereign power of which the kings had only dreamed'. The power wielded by a group, whether an aristocratic or parliamentary regime, may be as absolute as that of a king and the example of Cromwell shows that personal power does need to be monarchical.

Absolutism is, however, as a term used by historians to describe regimes of the sixteenth, seventeenth and eighteenth centuries, inextricably linked with monarchy. We may agree with Kossman that there was a general tendency for the state to expand its powers as the centre strove to exert its authority over provinces, towns and all competing authorities,

Figure 7
The Royal Gift of Healing
– Charles II touching for
the Evil, *engraving by Robert
White. Mansell Collection.*

and sought to extend its fiscal powers and jurisdiction. There was also a common need to do this: foreign policy, war and the very survival of the state demanded the efficient concentration of resources and, above all, the extraction of increased revenues from the population. The increased cost of warfare meant that those states which succeeded in increasing taxation throve and expanded their territories at the expense of those who failed to do so. It was thus foreign policy, and the cost of warfare, which largely dictated the attempts to centralize and standardize domestic government. But nearly all governments were monarchies and the heterogeneous nature of the possessions of monarchs represented acquisitions over time, the result of inheritance, marriages and successful wars. Their possessions, as we saw in Unit 1, were held under a variety of titles, some they ruled directly while others were under the direct control of powerful and largely autonomous vassals, and the institutions and administrations of territories were diverse. In seeking to unify such varied inheritances monarchs stressed the unique nature of monarchy and its right to absolute power. We must not forget that such power was not yet seen as entirely secular. Monarchs had a special relationship with God: they were anointed and their touch carried the gift of healing.

The monarchs of France and of the British Isles had the great advantage that their realms were geographically concentrated and largely co-terminous, even though the Stuarts ruled over three kingdoms and the Irish Sea provided a weak point. Both Bourbon and Stuart monarchs called upon the theory of absolute monarchy to support their aim of increased control of their inheritances.

France

The French monarchy has more than any other been seen as quintessentially absolutist and has provided the model for the concept. The reign of Louis XIV has for long been seen as the culmination of the tendency to absolute monarchy which had marked the reigns of his predecessors.

Exercise   I would now like you to read Offprint 17, pp.99–101 and then answer the following questions:

1   When did the term absolutism begin to be used to describe the seventeenth-century French monarchy?

2   Was the word always used to disparage the monarchical regime?

3   Why did it take so long for the accuracy of the concept of absolutism to be challenged?

Discussion   You would probably have noted the following.

1   The term began to be used at the very end of the eighteenth century after the French Revolution.

2   Although it was first used in pejorative way, some historians were soon using absolutism in a positive way. These later saw absolutism as a modernizing tendency which was opposed to aristocratic privilege.

3   Because historians of the national history of France tended to
     assume that the policies and commands of the centre were obeyed
     and didn't consult sufficiently the documentary evidence nor read
     the works of the historians of the French provinces.

You have been introduced to the concept of historical revisionism by
Anne Laurence in Unit 4 and are familiar with examples of the way
interpretations of the English civil war or Great Rebellion have recently
been revised. Roger Mettam, you will have realized by now, is a thorough-
going revisionist when it comes to French absolute monarchy. He dates
the beginning of the debate over the appropriateness of the term
absolutism from the publication of Roland Mousnier's book, *La Venalité
des offices sous Henri IV et Louis XIII* (1945) though, as we have seen, Kossman thought the term unchallenged in his 1976 publication nevertheless
conceding that if the term was not controversial, its meaning was.

A concept like absolutism is clearly vulnerable to revisionists
because, by its nature, it claims too much. No power in the real world can
be absolute in practice. What we have to decide is what was meant by
those who claimed absolute power for seventeenth-century monarchs and
how far that meaning became practice.

Exercise   1   Before turning to contemporary theory, let me ask what the concept
                  of an absolute monarch means to you?

             2   Can you think of synonyms for absolute monarchy?

Discussion 1   The obvious answer is the idea that there should be no limit to the
                  power of a king or queen.

             2   Words that come to my mind are 'despotism', 'tyranny' and 'dic-
                  tatorship' or 'monarchical dictatorship', perhaps even 'totalitarian-
                  ism'.

You probably silently qualified your answer to question 1 by adding 'in so
far as he or she was able in practice to exercise such unlimited power'.
With question 2 you may have been uneasy with supposed synonyms that
were drawn from either the classical or late modern worlds, rather than
from the period we are discussing; in this you would have been correct
for, as we shall see, contemporary proponents of absolute monarchy were
keen to distinguish between it and despotism and felt there should be
important limitations to the power of sovereigns.

The concept of absolute monarchy thus seems at first sight straightforward, the view that there should be no limit to the power of the king.
Jacques Bénigne Bossuet was one of the great theorists of the concept
and his *Politics Derived from Holy Scripture* was published in 1709. He wrote
that: 'The prince is accountable to none for what he commands ... When

the prince has pronounced a decision, no other decision can stand ... No other power can challenge that of the prince' (quoted in Henshall, 1992, p.131).

But Bossuet draws a distinction between *absolute* and *arbitrary* power: 'but it does not follow from this that the government is arbitrary since, besides everything being subject to the will of God, there are laws in states and anything done contrary to them is legally null' (quoted in Henshall, 1992, p.132).

It is important to stress that supporters of absolute monarchy were not defending something in being, but arguing for something they wanted to help bring about. They were well aware of the limitations of the power of kings and thought royal power should be greater. Their view of a king's authority did, however, stop well short of any idea of despotism or the modern concept of dictatorship.

Bossuet argued that the king's authority was absolute but at the same time, sacred, paternal and subject to reason. It was not *arbitrary.* The king's power was absolute under the laws of God and nature.

The obstacles to royal power

If the theory of absolute monarchy stopped well short of unlimited personal power, there were in addition many practical obstacles which prevented French kings from exerting their authority.

Exercise Read Briggs, pp.124–8 and 144–6 and answer the following questions.

1   Which group of officials does Briggs see as central to the 'administrative revolution' which enabled the royal income to be increased?

2   What was the main reason behind the need for increased revenue?

3   Does Briggs think that France became an absolute monarchy?

Discussion I would expect you to have noted the following.

1   The *intendants.* These special *commissaires* had by 1642 effectively replaced the old financial officials and had proved extremely efficient in supervising the collection of taxes.

2   The needs of modern warfare which was extremely expensive. Briggs sees the decision of Louis XIII and Richlieu to confront Spain as leading to administrative revolution and the increase in royal power exerted from the centre over the provinces.

3   Briggs is a bit ambivalent here. We are told that Richlieu's ministry heralded the great age of royal authoritarianism (note that Briggs does not hesitate to use the phrase 'royal despotism'). Yet after describing the consolidation of royal power with the personal rule of Louis XIV, he argues that Louis's 'absolutism' was 'often little more than a facade, behind which many of the old limitations continued to operate'.

The reasons Briggs gives for Louis XIV's success and for the continued limitations on his power are interesting. On the one hand he sees the king as 'bringing to climax an evolutionary process ... in which a combination of factors, including literary, printing and greater bureaucratic sophistication had allowed the monarchy to expand its power' (p.145). Further, he talks of the 'triumph of the centre over the periphery' (p.146). But he also agrees that the theory of absolute monarchy was qualified by a recognition that royal authority rested on religion and the laws of property. Louis placed voluntary limits on his power. In addition royal authority could not exercise constant control over the many levels of devolved power, partly because the bureaucracy was unequal to the task, and partly because by insisting on personal control the king and his ministers could only control so much.

Briggs writes of the 'great age of royal authoritarianism' (p.128) and comes close, despite his many qualifications, to accepting that an absolute monarchy was established in France. Mettam clearly holds the contrary view.

Exercise   Now read the rest of Offprint 17 and on the basis of this reading summarize the limits on royal power.

Discussion   You probably included some of the following in your answer.

1   No absolute ruler would have found himself or at least his officers in the law courts as much as did Louis XIV. As the crown sought to rationalize and standardize the administration of the kingdom, so established interests, subsidiary and provincial, challenged its right to override established rights and privileges. Even though, with the exception of seigneurial and municipal courts, justice was dispensed by royal judges, these judges proved to be very independent of ministers' wishes. At the highest level this led to disagreements between the chief judge, the king himself (the king personally exercised certain judicial functions such as the right to pardon), and those courts of appeal, the *parlements* and, especially, the most powerful *parlement* of Paris. On the whole, however, the king preferred to work with the *parlements* if he could. Such co-operation was, indeed, essential, for to have the force of law all royal edicts needed to be registered by the *parlements*.

2   There were difficulties in enforcing royal directives because those who were responsible for enforcing the law in the provinces were often in sympathy with those opposed to new taxes.

3   The clergy and the nobility could also oppose royal authority when it conflicted with their rights and privileges. The *noblesse d'épeé* were concerned to preserve their superiority to the *noblesse de robe* while the *princes étrangers* had interests in foreign affairs which could conflict with the king's foreign policy.

4   The French church might be Roman Catholic but the king was not always on good terms with the pope, while there were tensions and factions within the church and no clear agreement on the extent of papal and monarchical power. Most importantly there was the question of the Protestants. Both Huguenots and extreme Catholics could find religious reasons for defying royal authority.

You may also have noted further points, recalling that whereas Briggs sees a victory of the centre over the periphery, Mettam is pretty sceptical as to the centre's degree of success. Both agree, however, that there was a long struggle between a crown seeking to extend royal control and the groups and institutions which possessed special privileges grounded in law and tradition. Between 1661 and 1683 Jean-Baptiste Colbert attempted to build upon the achievements of Richlieu and Mazarin in extracting revenues from the French population but to avoid the arbitrariness and the venality of their methods.

Now cast your mind back to Unit 5: Louis, after Mazarin's death, was determined to rule without a chief minister but Colbert had responsibility for finance and administration. Colbert's plans for extending and reforming the monarchical administration were ambitious indeed. They went far beyond tax collection for he was an exponent of what in the twentieth century would be called central planning and was an early example of that love of symmetry and government control which has marked subsequent French administrations. He favoured state trading companies, protectionist tariffs, the promotion of new industries and other forms of state intervention.

Briggs comments that Colbert 'emerges as the practitioner of a kind of *dirigisme* which never worked out as he intended'. He sought to rationalize the tax system, wished to reduce exemptions and to eradicate corruption. From Colbert and from the centre came a stream of government plans, decrees and instructions; at the periphery they were met with opposition, obfuscation and delay. Yet Colbert enjoyed some success in the 1660s and might well have enjoyed more if peace had continued. The irony was that it was the desire to equip the state for war that necessitated high taxation and its efficient collection but it was the resumption of major wars in 1672 that destroyed Colbert's plans for reform and necessitated a return to short-term expedients.

Colbert realized the unpopularity of high taxation and knew that part of the popularity, which Louis enjoyed when he embarked upon his personal rule, rested upon the hope that the king's tax demands would be more moderate and more fair than those of the two great and greedy cardinals. For a while in the 1660s revenue and expenditure actually decreased but from 1671 there was a continuous and steep increase.

Exercise   I would like you to look at graphs 3, 4, 5 and 6 at the back of Briggs.

1   What do you think accounts for the sharp increase in revenues and expenditure?

2   How is the increase in revenue achieved?

Discussion   1   Clearly both increases were caused by Louis's wars. From 1672 to 1679 there was the Dutch War occasioned by France's invasion of the United Provinces, from 1689 the Nine Years' War and from 1701 to 1713 the War of the Spanish Succession.

2   It proved difficult to increase direct taxation, primarily the *taille*, and more indirect taxes which hit the aristocracy as well as peasants were in any case favoured by Colbert so that, until 1695, the main

increase was indirect taxation. After this, however, the needs of war forced a steep increase in other direct taxes while borrowing and the sale of offices were also resorted to.

You may also have noted that the graphs show that Colbert's efforts at reform of the royal finances enjoyed some success until the 1670s and that his achievements disappeared towards the end of the century.

The theatre of absolute monarchy

Whatever the practical limitations on his power, Louis XIV looked all powerful. His reign witnessed a sustained effort consciously to promote the image of a glorious and all-powerful king, a conqueror and patron of the arts whose semi-divinity was imparted via the classical tradition as much as by the Christian divine right of kings. Monarchy had always used ceremony and pageantry to support its sacerdotal claims and impress its earthly authority on subjects but with Versailles as the stage, the king's daily routine as the plot and far-off victories as the back-drop, Louis XIV's image was projected by elaborate theatre.

As you will recall from TV1 the theatre that was Versailles relied upon a clear language of architectural and pictorial symbols to transmit the message of absolute monarchy. Its importance can be measured in the amount of the national resources that it consumed and the man-hours and even lives of the soldiers who dug the canal to provide the water for its fountains and lakes (see Saint-Simon's comments on this in *Anthology*, III.8). But its purpose was not just to be magnificent and to over-awe. It was meant to be the setting for a court that for the aristocracy would not just be the centre of France but would embody France itself. The great aristocrats were tamed and domesticated by Versailles and the owners of impressive chateaux and great estates jostled for the honour of carrying a royal chamber pot. Army officers neglected their regiments and bishops their dioceses to attend the court. It was the only place to be.

Exercise   Read *Anthology*, III.8 and say what you think attracted the aristocracy to Versailles. (It is perhaps necessary to point out that, although Saint-Simon is a useful source, he was a man disappointed in his expectations of royal favour and as such was not the most impartial of observers.)

Discussion   The system hinged upon the idea of the king as the source of power and the head of society, yet the actual rewards and punishments he gave could seem slight to the outsider: to be seen to be intimate with his majesty or not to be recognized by him. The honour of being allowed to wear a royal jerkin is a case in point; it cost the king little but was of great importance to the wearer. (George III was to institute a similar system with the Windsor jacket which is still used today.) The whole court system was built upon such silken threads but proved strong enough to cage the French aristocracy.

LE LEVER DU ROY

Figure 8
Le Lever du Roi, *engraving of the first public scene of the daily ceremonial pageant of the court of Louis XIV. Mansell Collection. (You will also see a depiction of the Lever in TV1 in the tapestry of cardinal Quigi being presented to the king.)*

There were of course real rewards for enjoying the king's favour but what is impressive is the degree to which *social* rewards and penalties sufficed. At the 'court' of a great dictator of the twentieth century, like Joseph Stalin, men similarly hung upon his every word and were seen to be in or out as to whether they were invited to his *dacha* or not, but there the rewards and especially the penalties were serious indeed. But in the final analysis the competition for signals of royal favour, the right place at the *le petit lever,* the *premier entreé* or the *grand lever* (see Fig.8), was based upon something very serious, the view of the king as much more than the first among equals of medieval times, and as far above even the greatest noble.

The gulf between monarch and even the mightiest subject made the building of great palaces by noblemen or ministers a delicate, even a hazardous, matter. Kings sought to express the power of majesty in their palaces, grandees to project their wealth and status in theirs.

Video Exercise

I would like you to view Video 11 and then answer the following questions:

1   Can we discern a direct pattern of royal innovation followed by noble emulation?

2   What can we learn about the relationship between kings and their nobles and ministers from the video?

Discussion 1   No, the pattern is more complex than that. In the building of Versailles, Louis XIV (as we know from TV2 as well as Video 11) was much influenced by the example of Vaux-le-vicomte, the palace built for his minister, Nicolas Fouquet. The Earl of Kellie, who had been in charge of Charles II's rebuilding of Holyrood Palace, was influenced by Holyrood when he came to rebuild his own Kellie castle. So we find a king following the example of a minister, even to using the same architect, decorator and garden-designer, and a nobleman emulating his king.

2   We can conclude that a degree of loyal emulation was acceptable to monarchs but that too proud an assertion by a subject was not wise. Louis XIV may have admired Vaux-le-vicomte but Fouquet spent the rest of his days a prisoner. His fall was not, of course, due to the fact that he had built himself too magnificent a house but rather to Louis's growing distrust of his ambition and arrogance to which the magnificence of the palace contributed and perhaps confirmed. Charles II was less prickly than Louis about his status and the outward signs of the distance that lay between him and his nobles and ministers but Castle Kellie was, in any case, an example of a subject's emulation and emulation was acceptable within limits.

The distance between Louis and even the greatest nobles can be seen in the idea that because of divine right he was uniquely close to God. Consider La Bruyère's famous account of prayers in the royal chapel.

> The great persons of the nation assemble each day in a temple that they call a church. At the far end of this temple stands an altar consecrated to their God, where a priest celebrates the mysteries they call holy, sacred and fearful. The great ones form a huge circle at the foot of this altar and stand erect, their backs turned to the priest and the holy mysteries, their faces lifted towards their king who is seen kneeling in a gallery, and on whom they seem to be concentrating all their hearts and spirits. One cannot help but see in this custom a sort of subordination, for the people appear to be worshipping their prince while he in turn worships God. (quoted in Levron, 1976, p.134)

Yet the view that Louis XIV broke the independence of the aristocracy by holding them in a gilded cage has to be qualified. It was the wealthiest and most powerful section of the aristocracy which met this fate, the sort of men who had led the revolts against royal authority. The aristocracy was a very large group in French society and the great majority of them seldom came to court. Whether they were of the sword or the robe, they were necessary to the crown as *seigneurs* and administrators and, provided they were loyal, it was in the royal interest that they stayed on their estates and in their localities; they might be unsatisfactory agents of the royal government but they were indispensable.

Those who gained most from attendance at court were men who sought to rise to high positions in state service. For those who wished for advancement in the ministries, the army, the navy, the church or the court itself attendance on the king was very necessary. If the court was a gilded cage there were careers in it and via it.

Religion

Even without the Protestants, religion posed a problem for royal authority (see Offprint 17, Briggs, pp.161–5 and Unit 7). There was the question of papal as opposed to royal authority, the relationship between royal and ecclesiastical authority within France, and there were the Jansenists to whom Louis was strongly opposed. But disputes over the appointment of bishops and doctrinal issues within the Catholic church were minor issues from the point of view of royal pretensions compared to the existence of subjects who belonged to a different church.

Figure 9
Guy-Louis Vernansel,
Allegory of the Revocation
of the Edict of Nantes, c.
1685. Musée National du
Château de Versailles. Photo:
Réunion des Musées
Nationaux Documentation
Photographique.

In 1685 Louis XIV issued his Revocation of the Edict of Nantes. The Revocation expressed not only Louis's dislike of Protestantism but the view, widely shared by contemporaries, that communities with a different faith from their sovereign could not be properly loyal to him. The Revocation was not therefore simply a religious decision but a political one as well designed to strengthen crown and state.

Exercise   Please read the Edict of the king (*Anthology*, III.9) and answer the following questions.

1   What reasons does the king give for the Revocation?

2   Are the members of the PRR (Pretended Reformed Religion) given any options other than to convert to Catholicism?

Discussion 1   Louis claims that he is really fulfilling the wishes of his grandfather, who had issued the Edict giving toleration to Huguenots. Henri IV had meant the Edict to be only a temporary expedient until the time was right for the Protestants to rejoin the Catholic church. The Protestants have recently been returning to the church in large numbers so the time is now right to revoke the Edict.

2   Well the ministers can leave France within fifteen days but the rest are not to be allowed to leave and their only alternative to conversion is to stay but not practise their religion.

It is quite true that there had been many conversions from Protestantism but a great number of these had been achieved by bribery and coercion. In 1684 a general policy of forced conversions had been inaugurated.

Figure 10
Louis XIV as the conqueror of Heresy, *engraving by Elias Hainzelmann, 1686. Bibliothèque Nationale de France, Paris.*

The Revocation was very popular with French Catholics and with Catholic Europe but some 250,000 Huguenots emigrated and it had the effect of raising religious tensions throughout Europe and of re-creating a sense of Protestant solidarity. It had a considerable impact in Britain making Englishmen and Scotsmen even more suspicious of the Catholicism of James II.

Louis's wars

To make war and to expand the frontiers of France were the overriding aims of Louis XIV. In a sense this was hardly surprising. Warfare and foreign policy were of the very essence of kingship. How else did one become a glorious monarch save by success in war? We have seen that the desire for a more efficient administration, for the collection of greater revenues and for greater personal and central control over aristocracies, towns and provinces, features which distinguished seventeenth-century monarchies – were largely born of the need to fight wars. Louis was fortunate that the resources and conditions of France were such as to enable him to do so more effectively than anyone else.

As we have seen, Louis's wars did put a tremendous strain upon the resources of the state and upon the administration that harvested the resources of the state in the form of taxes, but, so long as his wars were

Figure 11
Portrait of Louis XIV,
victorious at Maastricht, by
Pierre Mignard, 1673, oil on
canvas. Pinacoteca, Turin.
Photo: Alinari.

successful, Louis appeared the epitome of a modern, glorious and absolute monarch.

Briggs's table (p.152) charts Louis's wars and we can see how successful he was during the first half of his reign. He was no dashing general (despite the statues and romantic murals), and as a tactician he was happier with a well-prepared siege than a daring attack but, as Colbert served him well in finance and administration, so Vauban served him in war.

By the late 1680s Louis appeared not only supreme at home but victorious abroad. If the Peace of Nijmegen with the United Provinces, Spain and the Holy Roman Empire did not give Louis all he wanted, it was broadly satisfactory, providing France with a more defensible northern frontier. Louis's gains were confirmed by the Truce of Ratisbon of 1684. With hindsight we can point to the disadvantages of his position: the strain of wars upon French finances as the benefit of Colbert's reforms was lost; the fact that French institutions and administration remained unreformed and inefficient; and the multitude of enemies which only lacked, as yet, the opportunity to become a great coalition. Few contemporaries saw this.

The Stuarts

For much of the seventeenth century many Englishmen believed that the Stuart kings were determined to introduce absolute monarchy on the French pattern. Coward (p.92) argues that neither James I nor Charles I claimed absolute power but 'acted within the common law and respected the inviolability and superiority of parliamentary statute'. But as we have seen, the kings of France also accepted that they should act within the law. There was no polarity between absolute and limited or mixed power. In both France and the British Isles there was widespread acceptance that the crown was sovereign *and* that subjects had rights. Stuart monarchs did argue for absolute monarchy. What they meant by it, however, was that kings had the final authority and could in an emergency override subordinate authorities, but should in general rule within the law. As James I put it: 'A king governing in a settled kingdom leaves to be a king and degenerates into a tyrant as soon as he leaves off to rule according to his laws …'. It was the *interpretations* of the law by Stuart kings that caused trouble, not a lack of respect for the law as such.

As we have seen, the urgent need of seventeenth-century governments was to maximize the potential of their dominions for war. It was this which lay behind the demand of both Bourbon and Stuart monarchs for greater power and in particular for greater revenues and for standing armies and strong navies. But the Stuarts operated in a different context from the kings of France. The Stuarts had some advantages: Britain and Ireland were geographically concentrated and protected by sea; England was a unified kingdom; and royal central authority was well established with little in the way of separate jurisdictions. On the other hand, Scotland was a distinct realm in a way beyond the limited autonomy of some of the possessions of the French kings. Ireland presented different problems again and, if it was far from a 'colonial society' (see Connelly, 1992), it was throughout the century subject to a determined effort to enforce royal authority via the imposition of an English system of land tenure, English and Scottish settlements and the replacement of its traditional Brehon law by English law.

Even what at first sight seemed advantages to British kings wishing to enhance their personal power in fact posed problems. The success of the monarchy in extending the crown's functions in England had been accomplished in conjunction with parliament and could not easily be taken further without parliament's agreement. There was no equivalent to this national assembly in France. John Miller (1990, p.195) has argued that monarchs owed whatever success they enjoyed in moving towards absolute monarchy: 'partly to the creation of cadres of officials committed to the extension of royal power, partly to the acceptance by other social groups that absolutism offered advantages, in terms of either profit or security'. English kings never managed to build up such a cadre of officials, while, because royal authority was strong in England to start with, the view that the king needed more power in order to bring competing and often arbitrary subordinate authorities to heel and to bring order to the inefficiencies of economic and political particularism failed to gain ground. There were thus structural and institutional obstacles to absolutism.

In Scotland the situation was very different. There central authority was weaker. Miller summarizes its weakness as follows:

> The great nobility wielded power reminiscent of that of English magnates of the late middle ages, their economic hold over the peasantry reinforced by their own law courts. The lesser landowners, the lairds, were in the Lowlands emancipating themselves from the tutelage of the magnates, but in the Highlands and Borders clan chiefs feuded and plundered largely unhindered by the king's government. The crown was wretchedly poor ... and its powers of coercion were correspondingly feeble ... Government was thus a matter of balancing magnate interests: the bloody deaths of so many Scottish kings showed how vulnerable the king's person was. (Miller, 1990, p.217)

Exercise Do you think Scotland offered a better or a worse breeding ground for absolute monarchy than England?

Discussion Probably in the hands of a capable king who understood the country well it offered a better potential. Enhanced royal authority could be seen as a way of putting an end to disorder and dissension in the interests of trade and prosperity.

Miller goes on to say (p.217), 'the institutional (as opposed to practical) obstacles to royal power were weak ... if the crown could control the magnates, and increase its powers of coercion, it might be able to extend its effective power much faster and further than would be possible south of the border'. Under James I, whom Coward calls 'the most competent king Scotland ever had' (p.120), royal power was cautiously and effectively extended but his successors lacked both his competence and his local knowledge.

The case of Scotland also highlights the great disadvantage James I's successors had compared to their Bourbon contemporaries. Their religious inclinations went against the grain of majority religious opinion in the greater part of their realms. This factor may well have been decisive in determining a more absolute monarchy for France and a less absolute one for Britain. The Stuart kings after James I seemed to have an atavistic tendency towards Catholicism, even if this was unfair to Charles I who remained a loyal member of the Church of England.

Their Catholic queens and alliances with Catholic powers provided not only the cause of many of their troubles but established in the minds of their subjects a link between absolutism and Catholicism. Within popular culture the beliefs that freedom and Catholicism were incompatible, while Catholicism and poverty went together – 'the pope and wooden shoes' – became deep-seated. James II's open Catholicism, together with his maladroit approach to the religious question, was to cost him the throne.

This denouement to the Restoration and to the reigns of Charles II and James II should not obscure the degree to which the British monarchy was actually stronger after the Interregnum, as was the French monarchy after the wars of the Frondes. This may seem obvious enough in the case of France but at best paradoxical in the case of the British Isles. A monarch must, one imagines, feel uneasy when his father and predecessor has been executed and he enters his inheritance after a period of republicanism and military rule. The institution of monarchy must surely have been damaged by its humiliations.

It is possible that Charles II did indeed feel uneasy, but that was because he overestimated the strength of his enemies, thinking that anti-monarchists and the Presbyterians and sects were much stronger than they were. This largely explains his caution in failing to reward adequately those who had been loyal to the Stuart cause and the fact that the Act of Uniformity expressed the wishes of parliament rather than the king.

The real strength of Charles II's position lay in the twin factors of the reaction to the events of the civil war and Interregnum and the legacy of Cromwell. The miscalculations of the parliamentary leaders of the 1640s had led to what few had wanted, a bloody civil war, the attempts at a 'Godly Reformation' and the abolition of the monarchy. If to moderate opinion in the early 1640s royal misrule had appeared a greater threat than disorder, by 1660 things were reversed and the monarchy seemed an essential guarantee of stability and a bulwark against the threat from religious and political radicals.

Figure 12
Charles II, *portrait attributed to Thomas Hawker, c.1680, oil on canvas, 226.7 cm x 135.6 cm. Courtesy of the National Portrait Gallery, London.*

Charles inherited from the Interregnum a more efficient system of taxation, a larger navy and a small standing army. His powers were defined by the Convention of 1660 and by the royalist 'Cavalier Parliament' elected in 1661. If there was to be no return to the fiscal devices of the 1630s nor to the Star Chamber, parliament dropped its pretensions to a share in the executive and there were no limitations on the king's right to control the army.

Exercise   Read Coward pp.289–92 and say why, although Charles inherited a position as *potentially* powerful as Louis XIV, he failed to realize that potential.

Discussion   I would expect you to have noted the following points.

1   Charles's personality and ability. The king had the great strength of seeing when he should give way and he was capable enough when it came to safeguarding his interests, but he lacked a consistent concentration upon policy objectives.

2   He didn't have the financial resources of Louis. Parliament was just not prepared to vote for high levels of taxation. Charles had, like his predecessors, an income for life that was supposed to be sufficient to meet normal peacetime expenditure, but most MPs were ignorant of the needs of public finance. Even if Charles had not been extravagant, the crown's revenue would have been inadequate to sustain government.

The enduring problem of Stuart monarchs was that they were perpetually hard up. There was no equivalent to the French *taille*, a permanent tax upon the main source of wealth, land. Charles was marginally better off than his predecessors but his policy-making was still heavily constrained by lack of money. There were improvements to the financial position during Charles's reign and by 1685 there was a national network of customs and excise officials, but the power of a basically wealthy state remained constrained by the reluctance of parliament to vote the king enough money.

As we have seen, Charles II underestimated his potential strength. There were risks involved in seeking a strong monarchy in alliance with a confessional state based on an exclusive Anglicanism, but the chances of success for such a policy were good. The sensible corollary in foreign affairs to such a domestic policy would have been one of caution and the avoidance of alliances with Catholic powers, which were likely to be unpopular with public opinion. When in 1670 he abandoned his support for religious toleration and took the Commons side in a dispute with the Lords, he found parliament conciliatory and prepared to provide new revenues.

Andrew Marvell wrote at the time that, 'no king since the Conquest [was] so absolutely powerful at home as he is at present' (Margoliouth, 1971, p. 315). Yet Charles was, at the same time, secretly pursuing an alternative and potentially unpopular policy.

After the failure of his first foreign initiative, the Second Dutch War, Charles embarked on the very foreign policy most likely to weaken his domestic position, an alliance with France. The Treaty of Dover of 1670 bound Charles to join France in a war against the Dutch Republic. Louis's motives in this alliance were obvious enough: the alliance broke up the Triple Alliance between England, Holland and Sweden that had followed the Treaty of Breda after England's defeat in the Second Dutch war; it also gave France a valuable ally. Charles's motives were a mixture of a desire for revenge for the humiliation of the battle of the Medway and the desire for the promise of help from France in the event of a rebellion at home.

In fact the alliance was more likely to weaken Charles's domestic position than to buttress it. The Dutch might be disliked as commercial rivals but they were at least Protestants and alliance with France was rarely popular in seventeenth-century England.

English opinion would have been more alarmed if it had become known that Charles had told Louis in 1669 that he wished to become a Catholic. As it was, opinion was outraged by the Declaration of Indulgence which the king issued in 1672 shortly before he declared war on the Dutch. The declaration, which was an extension of the royal prerogative, allowed Nonconformists to worship in public and Catholics in private. Nonconformists were more concerned at the toleration extended to Catholics than pleased at that extended to themselves. Fears about Catholicism mounted, when the conversion, to Catholicism, of the heir to the throne, Charles's brother, the Duke of York, was announced in 1673. Popery and its concomitant, French style absolute monarchy, seemed around the corner.

Parliament demanded that Charles revoke the Declaration of Indulgence and introduce a Test Act to exclude non-Anglicans from holding office and the king reluctantly agreed. By now England had joined Louis in his war against the Dutch and Charles needed money.

Exercise I would now like you to read *Anthology*, III.10, and then answer the following questions.

1   Is the Act even-handed as between Catholics and Protestant dissenters?

2   What was the main effect of the Act?

Discussion I would expect your answer to include the following.

1   Clearly as its sub-title implies, the Act was aimed primarily against Catholics.

2   Its main effect was to prevent all non-Anglicans from holding public offices.

The Act makes it clear that England was a confessional state (Scotland was too but under a different church) and if Catholics and Nonconformists were not actively persecuted they did not enjoy equal rights with Anglicans. As we have seen however, dissenting Protestants were more concerned with the threat from Catholicism than with their own disadvantages.

The Duke of York did not take the test required by the Act and in September 1673 he married Princess Mary of Modena, a Catholic. The king had no legitimate child so the possibility of a Catholic succession threatened. Parliament demanded that the marriage should not be consummated and there were assertions that the king's ministers were popish and dangerous. Suspicious of the king and opposed to the war, parliament refused to vote any more money. In February 1674 Charles made peace with Holland and then prorogued parliament.

Coward (p.318) comments: 'It is ironic that Charles's choice of policies that were (in part at least) aimed at strengthening the monarchy arguably delayed the creation of a strong monarchy for at least a decade. A Catholic heir and a pro-French foreign policy raised a barrier of mistrust between crown and parliament, ...'.

The feasible policy for Charles was, as it had always been the 'cavalier' policy of combining the considerable loyalty to the monarchy with support for the Church of England – and with a cautious foreign policy.

It was by following such policies that Charles survived the tumult of the hysteria of the Popish Plot and the threat of the Exclusion Crisis. This latter was caused by a series of attempts to have the Duke of York excluded from the succession. For the first time parliament was clearly divided between court and country parties, which became known as the Tory and Whig parties (Tory was the name for Catholic bandits in Ireland while Whig was an abbreviation of Whiggamore, extreme Presbyterian Covenanters in Scotland). The Whigs were successful in the elections to three successive parliaments between 1679 and 1681.

Charles's position was, however, essentially strong: few were, in the final analysis, prepared to plunge the country back into civil war; Scotland and Ireland gave little trouble and the Covenanters' rising of 1679 was easily put down; while, most importantly, the royal finances were in good shape. Historians who have concentrated upon opposition to the king in the Commons have been guilty of almost the ultimate anachronism by underestimating the importance of the Lords; the peers of England were of key importance both within and without their chamber and for the most part they backed the king. Charles, in short, had advantages which had been denied to his father.

Charles II ignored the Triennial Act while he and James II exercised tight control over the machinery of the law and of local government, appointing judges at pleasure, purging political opponents from county militias, the commissioners of the peace and borough corporations. They improved their financial position by reforming the Treasury and providing for direct administration of the revenues; this was to enable James to maintain a considerable standing army.

James II thus inherited a strong monarchy from his brother and despite all the fuss of the Exclusion Crisis his accession was both normal and peaceful. His promise to defend and support the Church of England went down well as did his undertaking to abide by the laws of England which he considered were 'sufficient to make the king as great a monarch as I can wish'. Parliament had not met since 1681 but James, by exerting every pressure and utilizing every means of patronage, ensured that the parliament which met in May 1685 was to his liking. The solidity of his position was tested by Monmouth's Rebellion and the lack of support for Monmouth among aristocracy and gentry confirmed James's security (see Unit 11). The great question is therefore how a king who seemed more powerful than his predecessors, who had a standing army, a compliant parliament and a good financial position, should within three years have fled his kingdom in ignominy.

The reasons for the Glorious Revolution

We have already outlined the traditional Whig view of 1688 which sees the revolution as the crucial event in a struggle for sovereignty between king and parliament which had been going on for most of the century. Marxists too see the revolution as part of a long-term development and as a sequel to a 'bourgeois English revolution', in which if the 'bourgeoisie' turn out to be rather aristocratic, the main outcome was the removal of barriers to the development of a more capitalist economy. They do not, however, attach major significance to 1688 seeing it more as a mere *coup d'état* against attempts to reverse an inevitable historical process.

Recent interpretations have tended to argue against long-term explanations, contending that hindsight has led to the imposition of patterns of development which are misleading in themselves, ignore the complexity of events and allegiances and neglect both short-term factors and the influence of accident and personality.

Charles and James had greatly augmented the scope of the crown, though arguments that they were close to establishing an 'absolute monarchy' run into the difficulties which, as we have seen, surround this term. Coward asserts that although James had an authoritarian temperament he did not intend to rule without parliament or to govern unconstitutionally. James's overthrow was caused by a combination of his religious policies, and the means by which he sought to implement them and his personal failings.

James was successful in increasing the extent of the royal prerogative so long as he had the support of the established church, the greater part of the aristocracy and the Tory gentry. When he lost that support, he was not deposed by his subjects but there was no substantial body of support to prevent William of Orange, the husband of his daughter, Mary, overthrowing him.

The Declaration for Liberty of Conscience of 1687 was only one among the many steps by which James attempted to improve the position of Catholics and to enable them to take prominent positions in the state, the army and the universities, but it was an important one and did much to cost him Tory and Anglican support. The Declaration can be seen as the attempt by a king whose own religious beliefs were shared by only a small fraction of his subjects to win toleration for his co-religionists and other non-Anglicans. To most of his Protestant subjects however it raised the question as to whether their king could be loyal to them.

Figure 13
William III, *detail of equestrian portrait by Sir Godfrey Kneller, oil on canvas. Royal Collection.* © *1994 Her Majesty Queen Elizabeth II.*

Exercise I would now like you to read *Anthology*, III.11.

1   How would you characterize the document?

2   How does it compare with Louis's Revocation of the Edict of Nantes?

3   How do you think it was received by James's subjects?

Discussion 1   The Declaration appears to be the epitome of toleration. It seems, especially as compared to the Revocation, to express the view that religious beliefs are essentially a personal matter and that people should neither be forced in matters of religion nor suffer disabilities for their beliefs. This was not a view shared by many contemporaries.

2 It seems to express an attitude to religion which is the direct opposite to that of the Revocation. The latter expresses the dominant contemporary view which is both opposed to religious toleration and sees religious dissent as incompatible with loyalty.

3 By the majority, with considerable suspicion. Why was James so eager to enable non-Anglicans to take up civil and military positions?

There was in all probability no dark plot to coerce the English into becoming Catholics. James probably did believe in something close to religious toleration, largely because he thought that without religious disabilities most of his subjects would in time convert to Catholicism; an optimistic belief given that Catholics were less than five per cent of the population. His policies were however maladroit. The fact that he was even-handed in giving Protestant dissenters the same toleration as Catholics did him no good as the former were suspicious of his motives. The Revocation of the Edict of Nantes had increased their fears that what was planned was the imposition of Catholicism. In 1688 James further aroused his Protestant subjects with a second Declaration of Indulgence and by taking action against the seven bishops who refused to read it from their pulpits.

James compounded his errors by inaugurating what was a sort of social and political revolution in the counties and boroughs of England. In order to make local government co-operative, he replaced members of the Tory and Anglican gentry and burgesses related to the gentry with dissenters and Catholics, many of them outsiders without the wealth, status and education of the traditional local élites. To change the laws on religion was one thing but to interfere with local hierarchies and interests was dangerous indeed and does much to explain why James found so little active support after William of Orange had landed.

Yet in the event, James could still have won in 1688. He had a standing army of about 40,000 men which far outnumbered William's forces. A small number of desertions caused the king to panic and he virtually gave up without a fight. The king's state of mind and the state of his health may have played a considerable part in the far from inevitable outcome.

Figure 14
Mary II, *after the portrait by William Wissing, 1685, oil on canvas, 124.5 cm x 100.3 cm. Courtesy of the National Portrait Gallery, London.*

The significance of 1688

How stands the Glorious Revolution now? Did it change the course of English and British history and save us from absolutism? Did it merely signify a change of monarch and leave Britain essentially an *ancien régime* society?

Exercise   The Bill of Rights or Declaration of Rights is often taken as a key document which testifies to the importance of the revolution. I would like you to read it (*Anthology*, III.12) and then answer the following questions.

1   Is this a revolutionary document?

2   What are the main charges laid against the conduct of James II?

3   What are the main liberties which the document asserts?

4   What limitations does it place upon the power of the monarch?

Discussion   1   Only in the contemporary sense of 'revolution' that the wheel goes full circle and returns to its original position. The document reiterates ancient rights embedded in existing law. It is also significant that the claim is that King James has abdicated; he has not, at least in theory, been expelled or overthrown.

2   The main charges come into two overlapping categories: that he attempted to subvert and extirpate the Protestant religion and the laws and liberties of the kingdom.

3   The rights of parliament, and legal liberties.

4   There is an assertion or re-assertion of parliament's rights as against those of the sovereign but what is new is that, not only shall only Protestants succeed to the throne but no king or queen shall marry a Catholic.

It should also be noted that there is some ambiguity as to the status of the document as, when William accepted the throne, he made no mention of it and gave only a general assurance to respect laws and liberties. Two things are, however, significant: no sovereign thereafter was a Catholic or married to a Catholic and parliament was transformed. W. A. Speck (1988, p.246) has argued that 1688 changed parliament: 'from an event into an institution …The permanence of parliament is what distinguished the limited monarchy which the Revolution established from the absolutism to which the Stuarts had aspired'. And yet, if we read William Blackstone, the great eighteenth-century theorist of the constitution, whose views were widely accepted, we find him saying: '… in the exertion of his lawful prerogative the king is and ought to be absolute; that is so far absolute that there is no legal authority which can delay or resist him' (Blackstone, 1796, p.284).

The paradox at the heart of the events of 1688 is that the limitations that were placed upon the British monarchy came into being alongside a Protestant monarchy with an anti-French foreign policy, while it was a Catholic monarch and a pro-French foreign policy which had made them necessary. The prerogatives of the monarch in respect to war and foreign policy remained intact and these were what mainly mattered to monarchs, provided sufficient revenue was forthcoming. William found it much easier to gain money for his wars than his predecessors because his policies went with the grain of aristocratic, gentry and merchant opinion.

Scotland and Ireland and the Glorious Revolution

The crucial events of the Glorious Revolution took place in England. Scotland and Ireland reacted in 1689 to what had happened in England the previous year. That reaction does much to deny the bloodless reputation of the revolution for William had to crush James's supporters in Scotland by force of arms and had to fight a fierce and lengthy war in Ireland to establish his rule.

James had personal experience of Scotland where he had been, as Duke of York, virtual governor between 1679 and 1682. Besides putting down the Covenanters' revolts, he had promoted stability, the development of Scottish institutions, such as the Royal College of Physicians, and carried out his brother's policy of strengthening a comprehensive Episcopalian church. His position in Scotland was strong and, apart from a minority of extreme Presbyterians, the Scots were loyal to him at the beginning of his reign. Argyll's rebellion of May 1685 collapsed from lack of support.

James forfeited much of that support with measures favouring Catholicism and then brought in a Declaration of Indulgence which extended toleration to Covenanting Presbyterians. The sum of his efforts was to undermine the episcopacy with the result that he lost the full support of Episcopalians in the Church of Scotland and the landowners while, with the Revolution, the Covenanting Presbyterians took the opportunity to combine support for William with the overthrow of the established ecclesiastical order.

'In Scotland as elsewhere', J. C. D. Clark (1993, p.230) has commented, 'the Glorious Revolution owed its success to militant armed minorities'. The minority in question was an extreme group of zealots, known as the Cameronians after Richard Cameron one of their leading preachers. They had remained disaffected after the defeat of the Covenanters at the battle of Bothwell Brig in 1679 and, when the supporters of James II seceded from the Scottish Convention which met in May 1689, it was the Cameronians who defended it, and who checked the advance of James's supporters at Dunkeld after Viscount Dundee's victory at Killiecrankie. Scotland was to remain deeply divided between a Whig–Presbyterian ascendancy on the one hand and Episcopalians and Catholics on the other, and between the Lowlands and Highlands. Much of Scotland was to provide the basis of support for the Stuart cause with the establishment of a garrison at Fort William bearing testimony to divided loyalties.

It was, not surprisingly, in Ireland that James found his greatest support. The Earl of Tyrconnel had by 1688 disarmed the Protestant militia and purged the army of Protestants while almost the entire administration was composed of Catholics. When, in February 1689, James landed in Ireland he was met by Tyrconnel and almost the entire country was in his hands. The 'Patriot' parliament which met in Dublin in May 1689 declared the legislative and judicial independence of the country and restored estates taken from Catholic landowners in the previous half century.

It was to take William some two and a half years of campaigning to subdue Ireland, campaigns marked by Colonel Kirke's relief of Londonderry in July 1689, William's victory at the Battle of the Boyne in July 1690 and the surrender of Limerick on 3 October 1691.

Figure 15
The Siege of Londonderry,
*1688–9, engraving by
Adriaan Schoonbeeck (1657–
1705). Mansell Collection.*

The Treaty of Limerick provided for limited religious toleration for Catholics and protection for Catholic property but, even if William had wished to honour it, the English parliament had pre-empted him by repealing the legislation of the 'Patriot' parliament and imposing an Anglican test upon office-holders and the parliament that met in Dublin in October 1692 was a purely Protestant and largely Anglican assembly.

The ironic final outcome of James's religious policies was thus a Presbyterian establishment in Scotland and an Ireland ruled, not by a Protestant, but by an Anglican ascendancy.

The monarchies of France and the British Isles, 1688–1715

France was the dominant European power of the seventeenth century challenged only by Spain and the Empire. England by comparison was a secondary power. This was in large part, as we have seen, because French kings were much more successful in mobilizing the resources of their domains. After 1688 England became truly a great power with a navy which rivalled that of France, an army capable of effective intervention on the continent and an exchequer able to sustain allies as well as finance her own war efforts.

Two factors account for the increase in British power. In the first place England developed into what Brewer (1989) has termed a 'military fiscal state'. The cost of William's military adventures was considerable. By 1697 the army numbered some 76,000 men and the war budget was more than five million pounds. Queen Anne's wars were to be almost as expensive. To meet such a burden taxes had to be increased and the tax burden, extended. Duties from customs and excise actually declined in time of war and a land tax falling upon assessed rental values was introduced at a rate of four shillings in the pound. Even this was not enough and the Treasury resorted to borrowing – the National Debt was born. The funding of public credit brought into being a whole new financial world: the Bank of England, funds in which individuals invested capital, even government lotteries. Of course the high taxes were not popular, especially with landowners, and the Act of Settlement of 1701 was especially designed to control the capacity of foreign-born kings to involve the country in wars; but taxation continued and was efficiently collected. Nor were the *nouveaux riches* speculators who seemed to be doing well at the expense of landed gentlemen popular, but then there is rarely a better of sign of dynamic economic change than complaints about money getting into the wrong hands.

The second factor strengthening Britain was the emergence of a British state instead of two kingdoms joined by allegiance to the same crown. The first four Stuart kings had ruled Scotland separately from England. After James VI they had not done so with much skill and again religious policies had been at the root of most of their problems. Both James VI and Charles II had sought a peaceful union of the kingdoms but the attempts had failed largely due to English suspicions. Although the problem of the multiple kingdoms proved so disastrous for Charles I, only Cromwell attempted, successfully, to use the superior resources of England to impose English rule. William's invasion of England drove out the king of England but what of the king of Scotland? As we have seen, William was accepted by the Scottish Convention but it was, at least legally, an entirely separate matter to his accession to the English throne.

Although Scotland was more and more influenced by English military and economic power after 1688, there were at the same time strenuous assertions of Scottish independence: the Claim of Rights was the equivalent of the Declaration of Rights but was more forthright in what was claimed as subjects' rights. The dependence of the crown upon Presbyterian votes in the Scottish parliament and the association of Episcopalianism with the Stuart cause resulted in a Presbyterian settlement with less religious toleration than in England.

When the English parliament vested the succession in the House of Hanover, the question of Scotland's right to choose a different ruler arose. Many Scots felt that William had treated them badly for if he had been indifferent to English interests, he had totally ignored Scotland's. There was also considerable discontent over English protectionism which placed obstacles in the way of Scottish trade and in particular over the supposed English role in the Darien fiasco (the Company of Scotland's ill-fated attempt to establish a trading depot at Darien in Panama). Whether it was practical politics for Scotland to choose a different monarch from England was one question; whether there was a suitable candidate available was another; the Protestant who had the best legal title, the Duke of Hamilton, was not otherwise very suitable.

Exercise   Read *Anthology,* III.13.

    1   What English Act does the Act Anent Peace and War bring to mind?

    2   Summarize the meaning of the Act for the security of the kingdom.

Discussion   1   It has similarities to the Act of Settlement which was also largely occasioned by concern at the casual way William had engaged in war for mainly Dutch interests, taking his subjects willingness for granted.

    2   If Queen Anne died childless, the estates would choose her successor, who would only be the same as her successor in England if Scotland's independence, the freedom of its parliament, its religion and trade were protected.

Yet only three years later the Act of Union was passed. It can be argued that the Act of Union was actually pragmatic recognition of reality. In practice Scotland was already less than an independent kingdom but much more than a province. The Scots kept their established Presbyterian Church, their legal system and their educational system (note how the Scottish universities are all mentioned by name in the Act), and the rights of the royal Scottish burghs were to be safeguarded. Forty-five members of the House of Commons were to be representatives of Scottish seats which was ungenerous in terms of proportion of population but generous in economic terms (the ratio of MPs was 12:1, the population ratio 5:1 and the ratio of economic strength 38:1 (see Brown, 1992, pp.188–9); while sixteen Scottish peers were to sit in the Lords, which doesn't seem very generous, though many Scottish peers were soon made peers of Great Britain.

The two factors were probably decisive in securing Scottish assent to the union, the economic advantages of free trade with England (and the threat to the cattle trade if the act was not passed) and the guarantee of the 1690 church settlement. Although there were riots in Dundee and Glasgow and substantial opposition from the nobility, the excitement aroused by such a momentous decision can be exaggerated:

> Sovereignty alone was not a sufficiently popular cause to arouse the people to take up arms, and in 1706–7 the great majority even of the political élite did not bother to register their views. Three-quarters of the burghs and two-thirds of the shires did not petition at all. (Brown, 1992, p.190)

Great Britain was not to be made overnight but in the course of the eighteenth century a British identity was to be forged (see Colley, 1992) out of a common Protestantism, shared wars against the French, colonies and economic success.

The military fiscal state of Britain which the Hanoverians were to inherit was to be a formidable European power which the multiple kingdoms of the earlier Stuarts had never been. It would be misguided to underestimate the continued power of the crown, both as against the powers of Commons and Lords and within them, but Great Britain was no absolute monarchy. British monarchs ruled rather than merely reigned but did so in conjunction with a powerful aristocracy and with the need for support from gentry and mercantile interests. Problems remained: historians have, of late, argued that Jacobitism attracted considerable support even in the south of England while, if Ireland was quiescent under a Protestant ascendancy, it could not be relied upon to remain so in the event of war or Jacobite rebellion. But the military-fiscal state of Britain had an economic dynamism and a military potential that relative to size and population exceeded that of France.

Briggs (p.206) writes of France that:

> From a Renaissance state very similar to her neighbours the country developed into a distinctive 'absolute' monarchy which was widely admired and copied. At the same time social and economic relationships hardened into a mould which proved peculiarly durable, so that on most fronts the potential for further change was artificially restricted.

As we know all too well, there are problems with the term 'absolute monarchy' both as to its theory and the degree that theory could be put into practice. There can be no doubt however that Louis's personal power was enormous and that he had no institution to reckon with comparable to the English parliament. If both France and Britain had regimes which accepted the sovereign authority of the crown and the rights of the people, it was the authority of the crown which was more pronounced in France. Intermediate powers still existed in France as did regard for ancient rights and the rule of law but their residual strength lay in their ability to obstruct rather than play a positive role.

France, like Britain, was an aristocratic society and the king never tried to govern without the privileged orders. The idea that an absolute monarchy inaugurated a new bourgeois administration of royal servants is a myth for most of the higher bureaucrats were noble and it became progressively more difficult for new men to join their ranks. In contrast to the British Isles where the monarch ruled with the aristocracy, Louis ruled via the aristocracy.

Differences between the French and British aristocracies were in any case considerable. There were only some two hundred peers in eighteenth-century Britain and all the rest of the so-called aristocracy were technically commoners whereas there were thousands of French nobles. They constituted an estate with many legal privileges such as exemption from direct taxation while English peers had few legal privileges. The British aristocracy, as it was already becoming before the Act of Union, was prepared to tax itself as can be seen by land taxes; aristocrats were for the most part prepared to play their part, alongside the gentry, in the administration of their counties and were interested in improving their financial position by improving their land and even exploiting its mineral deposits. Whether the English aristocracy constituted an open élite has been questioned but they certainly mixed and inter-married with gentry families and were rarely without contacts with the professions and commerce. Both aristocracies were happy enough to seek wealth and power via court connections and public offices but the French nobility had a much smaller share in government and saw their interests as opposing change and reform rather than guiding and benefiting from them.

As we can see from Briggs's table (p.152), the wars of the latter half of Louis's reign were unsuccessful and France's frontiers were pushed back. The wars were also very expensive and punished the French economy at a time when agricultural productivity seems to have been decreasing and industry and commerce stagnating. If part of the problem was high taxation the other was excessive direction from the centre, a direction that often failed to be implemented. The fiscal-military state of Britain was an expanded state but one which rested firmly on an appreciation of local interests and respect for local power.

No doubt the old Whig view of the enormous significance of the Glorious Revolution in marking a parting of the ways between France and the British Isles exaggerated the importance of 1688 and the degree of difference between eighteenth-century Britain and France. Historians have of late tended to stress the continuity of British society and politics and to deny that the so-called revolution amounted to much more than a change of king. The power and influence of the monarchy in the eighteenth century is stressed as is the confessional nature of the British state. With its monarchy, aristocracy and established churches, Britain, it is suggested, was, like France, an *ancien régime* society (see Clark 1985, 1986; and on the king's role in foreign policy Black, 1985).

Yet, if much of the revisionist case can be accepted, Britain was in the early eighteenth century a society less constrained by rank and with a greater equality before the law than was France and most other European societies. In the economic sphere Britain exhibited a greater dynamism based on economic individualism and an absence of restraints on trade. There was in Britain a substantial middle to society and an emergent polite society that encompassed both wealthier merchants and gentry (see Langford, 1989). There was also parliament. It is among the paradoxes and the conflicting interpretations of eighteenth-century Britain that any continuing case for the long-term significance of 1688 has to be made.

References

Black, J. (1985), *British Foreign Policy in the Age of Walpole*, John Donald, Edinburgh.

Blackstone, W. (1765), *Commentaries on the Laws of England*, Oxford.

Bossuet, J.B. (1709), *Politics derived from Holy Scripture*.

Brewer, J. (1989), *The Sinews of Power*, Unwin Hyman, London.

Brown, K.M. (1992), *Kingdom or Province? Scotland and the Regal Union 1603–1715*, Macmillan, Basingstoke.

Clark, J.C.D. (1985), *English Society 1688–1832*, Cambridge University Press, Cambridge.

Clark, J.C.D. (1986), *Revolution and Rebellion*, Cambridge University Press, Cambridge.

Clark, J.C.D. (1993), *The Language of Liberty*, Cambridge University Press, Cambridge.

Colley, L. (1992), *Britons Forging the Nation 1707–1837*, Yale University Press, New Haven.

Connelly, S.J. (1989), *Religion, Law and Power: The Making of Protestant Ireland, 1660–1770*, Oxford University Press, Oxford.

Daly, J. (1978), 'The idea of Absolute Monarchy in Seventeenth Century England', *Historical Journal*, XXI, pp.227–50.

Hatton, R. (ed.) (1976), *Louis XIV and Absolutism*, Macmillan, London.

Henshall, N. (1992), *The Myth of Absolutism*, Longman, London.

Kossman, E.H. (1976), 'The singularity of absolutism', in R. Hatton (ed.), *Louis XIV and Absolutism*, Macmillan, London.

Langford, P. (1989), *A Polite and Commercial People*, Oxford University Press, Oxford.

Levron, J. (1976), 'Louis XIV's courtiers', in R. Hatton (ed.), *Louis XIV and Absolutism*, Macmillan, London.

Macaulay, T.B. (1906), *History of England*, vol.1, Everyman edition, London. (First published 1849.)

Margoliouth, H.M. (ed.) (1971), *Poems and Letters of Andrew Marvell*, vol.2, edited by H. M. Margoliouth, Oxford University Press, Oxford.

Mettam, R. (1990), 'France', in J. Miller (ed.) (1990), *Absolutism in Seventeenth Century Europe*, Macmillan Education, Basingstoke.

Miller, J. (1986), *Bourbon and Stuart*, George Philip, London.

Miller, J. (ed.) (1990), *Absolutism in Seventeenth Century Europe*, Macmillan Education, Basingstoke.

Mousnier, R. (1945), *La Ventilaté des offices sous Henri IV et Louis XIII*.

Speck, W.A. (1988), *Reluctant Revolutionaries. Englishmen and the Revolution of 1688*, Oxford University Press, Oxford.

Trevelyan, G.M. (1944), *English Social History*, Longmans, London.

Unit 13
Commentators on the state

Prepared for the course team by
Lucille Kekewich and Antony Lentin

Contents

Study timetable

Weeks of study	Texts	Video	AC	Set books
2	*Anthology*, III.15–30 and II.3 Offprint 18		AC2, section 5	Coward, Briggs

Objectives

The objectives of this unit are that you should:

1   understand and appreciate the main arguments of both the defenders and the opponents of absolute royal power in France and the British Isles;

2   understand why and how an increasing number of the monarchs' subjects, including some of the common people, attempted to secure a voice in national affairs.

Introduction

(Lucille Kekewich)

Blocks 1 and 2 charted the upheaval in the societies of the British Isles brought about by the civil wars and the crisis of 1688 and the way in which a potentially revolutionary situation in France occurred and was finally controlled. The question has arisen, implicitly or explicitly: were the participants in these stirring events working to a pre-conceived plan or did they happen accidentally, owing to the unique conjunction of a number of factors? This question echoes a recurrent problem about the interpretation of political ideas. Do the influential participants in great movements and events act in conformity to a predetermined set of beliefs about how the state should be governed? Or, are they borne along by the force of circumstance, self-interest or loyalty to the dominant value system and produce an ideological justification for their actions?

Those who see political ideologies in the first way, as having an existence above and apart from contemporary circumstances, will impute them primarily to an élite of philosophers and theologians. They will account for the ideas of thinkers such as Hobbes or Fénelon by concentrating almost exclusively on what they wrote. Pocock (1987) and Skinner (1978), on the other hand, incline to the view that political ideas develop as a pragmatic reaction to a particular sequence of events. The prevalent value system of society and the language in which it is expressed are closely associated with these ideas. As Skinner puts it:

> … I take it that political life itself sets the main problems for the political theorist, causing a certain range of issues to appear problematic and a corresponding range of questions to become the leading subjects of debate … it is evident that the nature and limits of the normative vocabulary available at any given time will also help to determine the ways in which particular questions come to be singled out and discussed. (Skinner, 1978, p.xi)

Most histories of political ideas published before the 1960s tended to confine investigation almost exclusively to canonic works: appropriate selections of the writings of the great philosophers. Skinner's view of political theory, on the other hand, involves a consideration of not only the intellectual inheritance of the writers but also of the contemporary influences to which they were subject. In some parts of this unit we incline towards Skinner's approach, not only will the works of political thinkers be studied, but also wider developments in government and society and popular reactions to them (the latter would not, until recently, have been considered to merit a place in a serious study of ideas). This has the advantage of enabling us to look much further down the social scale at the political attitudes and ideologies of men and women than is possible when research is confined to canonic works, the products of an educational and social élite.

France: authority and subversion

At the beginning of our period England had experienced more than fifty years of internal stability and order: France between 1560 and 1595 had by contrast been shaken by the Wars of Religion. Those of you who have studied A205, *Culture and Belief in Europe, 1450–1600*, will remember that these wars provoked all the major protagonists to justify their particular political objectives. The Huguenots defended their resistance to the royal government in books such as François Hotman's *Franco-Gallia*, by claiming that the king's authority, if it was exercised unlawfully, did not have to be obeyed. Hotman believed that natural law devolved the right to rule (sovereignty) onto an assembly of the people. The anonymous author of *The Defence against Tyrants* agreed, and claimed that a prince who exercised authority unlawfully violated the contract by which the subjects of their country's first ruler had originally agreed to entrust themselves to the care of his dynasty. The violation absolved his subjects from any duty to obey him, and legitimized his overthrow. The idea of a contract which preceded the exercise of sovereignty remained an important theme in the development of political ideas throughout the seventeenth and eighteenth centuries.

When the Huguenot leader, Henri of Navarre, succeeded to the throne as Henri IV in 1594, it was the Catholics, led by the formidable Catholic League, who adopted similar theories to justify their resistance to the 'heretic'. Jean Bodin and his kind were known as *politiques*, moderates who shunned the extremes of the religious antagonists. They produced an alternative view of sovereignty supporting the power of the king, whoever he might be, by enhancing his authority in every possible way. No lawful resistance could be offered to him, advisers could warn and remonstrate but, eventually, the whole nation should obey the royal will. Any other course would lead back to the dissolution of social order which had been such a traumatic experience during the Wars of Religion. Bodin's writings were known in England; early in the seventeenth century an English translation was made of his major work, *The Six Books of the Republic*. His view of royal power was to be influential both on the apologists for the absolutist aspirations of the Bourbons and on the defenders of an unfettered royal prerogative in Britain.

The early decades of the seventeenth century in France saw little activity by political theorists. The majority of Frenchmen shunned anything that might provoke civil conflict and were seemingly content with the *politique* formula of unquestioned royal sovereignty. The beleaguered Huguenots had the theories of resistance, discussed above, available to them. Yet despite the provocation offered by Louis XIII and Richelieu in attacking and destroying their strongholds in the 1620s, they were unwilling to mount a theoretical challenge to royal power. One historian, Ligou, accuses them of intellectual defeatism: they tended to present themselves as being even more loyal to the monarchy than the Catholics (Ligou, 1968).

The *Nu-pieds* produced some justifications of their defiance of royal authority during their revolt in Normandy in 1639. It was one of a number of revolts that occurred in France during this period, it happens to be unusually well documented because Chancellor Séguier, who kept a journal, went to suppress it.

Exercise Read the poems in *Anthology*, III.15 (A) and (B). Note that they were originally circulated in print but now survive only in manuscript.

1   What were the main grievances?

2   What remedies were proposed?

3   Do the poems contain any evidence for a political programme which went beyond the redress of immediate grievances?

Discussion 1   The strict imposition of the *gabelle* or salt tax was the main pre-occupation in both poems, but the condemnation entailed references to other grievances: the treachery, arrogance and luxurious life style of the tax farmers and their friends and the oppression felt by the people under a tyrannous regime: 'The Manifesto' associated tyranny with impiety. 'To Normandy' accused the government of ingratitude towards a province which had always been one of its strongest supporters. It went on to blame not only the tax farmers but:

The Cardinal and armies take
Our riches, goods, all we possess
And leave us in profound distress.

2   Violent measures were proposed to rectify the abuses of government in both poems, indeed they seem to have been printed and circulated mainly to raise men to fight for the *Nu-pieds*. Appeals were made to the various towns in Normandy and, in 'The Manifesto', to the people of Paris and to Bretons as well as to courtiers. The request to the nobility for support in 'To Normandy' was rather more subtle. The author played on the insults they had suffered, the threat to their status and the loss of their goods; all these problems would be solved if the rising succeeded.

3   'Programme' would be too ambitious a description of the remedies for Norman grievances offered in the poems. In some respects the thinking was traditional. The assumption that the tyrannous royal government was impious and that the rebels were on the side of the angels, seems to hark back to the polemical debates of the Wars of Religion. Beyond the immediate desire to destroy the tax farmers there was a general dissatisfaction with the government. The king was never mentioned but his minister was condemned in 'To Normandy'. Both poems promised liberty (at this time equated with the full enjoyment of local privileges) as the reward of a successful revolt: as it failed we will never know where such thinking would have led. It could not, however, have been easily accommodated within the strong, centralized monarchical state that Louis XIII and Richelieu were in the process of creating.

Some innovative political thinking can be found in Richelieu's justification for his policies, unimpeded as he was by any concern for the lower classes as a distinct entity within the state. In a memoir to Louis XIII, Richelieu wrote:

> ... they are often sensitive to and complain of necessary evils as readily as those which may be avoided, and they are as ignorant of what may be useful to a state as they are excitable and quick to bewail the ills they must endure in order to avoid greater ones. (Church, 1972, p.204)

From the mid-1620s Richelieu had energetically pursued the interests of the monarchy by a strong anti-Habsburg policy abroad and the suppression of the power of the nobility and the Huguenots at home. The necessity for such actions had been anticipated in the writings of Machiavelli, a century earlier, in his development of the concept of 'reason of state'. This allowed a government to override the standards of law and morality required of private people, when to do so would be to secure a result which would be in the interests of religion and the state. Bodin and Montaigne had, to some extent, envisaged this as a logical consequence of their desire for an omnipotent monarch, but both writers had quailed at the amoral consequences of the idea. Richelieu had no difficulty in finding defenders of his vigorous promotion of royal power: apart from self-interest, they probably represented the view of the majority of subjects that this was infinitely preferable to a reversion to the anarchy of the Wars of Religion. Guez de Balzac wrote *The Prince* in 1631. It provided a full justification for an unfettered exercise of sovereignty which was typical of the stance taken by a number of contemporary writers.

Exercise   Read *Anthology*, III.16 and then write a paragraph on how it supports 'reason of state'.

Discussion De Balzac invoked 'prudence', a higher authority even than 'justice', which could provide the most effective protection for the long-term interests of the state. He conceded that this might involve suffering but defended the policy on the grounds that the king did not spare himself in pursuit of the welfare of his subjects and did not lightly inflict hardships on them. When it was necessary for the good of the community, such privations had to be accepted.

The defence of Louis XIII's claims to exercise absolute power did not go unquestioned. Mathieu de Morgues, a pamphleteer who had previously supported Richelieu, took up the cause of Marie de Medici and Gaston d'Orléans. From the safety of the Cévennes he launched an outspoken attack.

Exercise   Read *Anthology*, III.17 (A) and (B). Compare them with *Anthology*, III.16.

     1   On what grounds was Richelieu condemned?

     2   What view emerges of 'reason of state'?

Discussion   1   In the second extract Richelieu was accused of preferring war with its attendant evils to peace. He was also called avaricious, ambitious and violent. It was implied that he had allowed the army and royal finances, as well as the king's poor subjects, to decline into a dangerously low condition. In the first extract de Morgues meant Richelieu and his followers when he accused those about the king of preventing him from receiving sound advice by charging those who offered it with the crime of 'lèse majesté': the cardinal behaved as if his own wishes were synonymous with those of the king.

           2   The view of 'reason of state' practically contradicted the Machiavellian account given by de Balzac. Louis was urged in the first extract to wield '… the sword of justice' and embrace the traditional Christian virtues of a king '… kindness, clemency …', to consider the misery of his people who had been sacrificed by those who dominated his affairs. In the second extract he was urged to call to his side those who had a 'natural right' to be near him (Gaston d'Orléans and the Queen Mother), God would bless him with peace at home and abroad. These proposals turned back the clock and required the kind of monarchical virtues which had been praised by moralists since the early middle ages.

None of the opposition to the extensive authority exercised by Louis XIII and his minister carried much conviction. While Gaston d'Orléans was heir to the throne his supporters' appeal to traditional kingly virtues might make some impact on the few people who read these pamphlets. The ill-formulated demands of the *Nu-pied* rebels and the ineffectual protests of the Huguenots would receive no sympathy from any Catholic prince. The apologists for strong, centralized royal authority were vindicated by the ability of the king and cardinal to control the forces which were to break out in the Frondes soon after they died.

The British 'Empire'

Despite the predominantly peaceful condition of English society during the reigns of Elizabeth I and James VI and I, pressure from religious activists was a perpetual source of aggravation. Both saw that attempts by Puritan religious leaders and politicians to achieve radical changes in the Anglican church could prejudice their prerogative. Many of the Puritans had links with continental Calvinists and the ideas of writers such as Hotman were well known to them. Whilst a body of such resistance literature existed to justify defiance of state religious policy, the rejection of arbitrary taxation also depended on home-grown legal and political traditions.

By the early decades of the seventeenth century lawyers and antiquaries had developed an idealized view of England's past. They believed that the Anglo-Saxons had enjoyed legal rights and possessed representative institutions which had enabled them to resist unreasonable encroachments by the royal prerogative. During the civil war and Interregnum, radical thinkers claimed that the Norman Conquest had introduced the autocratic rule of a series of kings who had tried to curtail the liberties of their 'free-born' subjects, and impose the 'Norman yoke' upon them (Pocock, 1987).

The relative harmony of Elizabeth's reign had set up another yardstick by which the Stuart monarchs were to be judged and censured. The rule of England, Wales, Ireland and later Scotland and the New England and Virginia settlements was Imperial, owing no allegiance to an external power. This idea was encapsulated in the *Britannia* of the antiquary William Camden:

> The King [hath] soveraigne power and absolute command among us, neither holdeth he his empire in vassallage, nor receiveth his investiture or enstalling off another, ne yet acknowledgeth any superior but God alone. (Camden, 1610, p.163)

This pride in England's strong and independent institutions could cause annoyance and even political danger to the Stuart kings. It was all very well for the antiquary, Sir Robert Cotton, to collect ancient documents about the English constitution (many of them filched from government archives). When he and like-minded friends used them to support arguments in parliament in favour of maintaining English 'liberties' against royal encroachment, the monarchy felt threatened. Early in his reign James I seems to have let it be known that he wished the Society of Antiquaries to suspend its activities.

King James himself made a substantial contribution to one view of the proper location of sovereignty within the state. Just before he ascended the English throne, in 1598, he had published *The True Law of Free Monarchies*:

> ... when the Bastard of Normandy came into England and made himself king, was it not by force and with a mighty army? Where he gave the law and took none; changed the laws; inverted the order of government; set down the strangers, his followers in many of the old possessors' rooms, ... And yet his successors have with great happiness enjoyed the Crown to this day. (Hughes, 1980, p.27)

Throughout the work he made it clear that the only person who enjoyed freedom under such a regime was the monarch who could do what he liked. James was, in fact, much more inclined to compromise with his English subjects than his theorizing would lead us to expect: he had gained plenty of experience in dealing with the formidable Scots nobility and clergy, who had no time for kingly pretensions to absolute authority. Yet when he did confront parliament he was still inclined to assert that his patriarchal view of royal power should be unquestioned:

> There be three principal similitudes that illustrates the state of monarchy: ... In the Scriptures kings are called gods and so their power after a certain relation compared to the divine power. Kings are also compared to fathers of families for a king is truly *Parens Patriae* [father of his country], the politic father of his people. And lastly, kings are compared to the head of this microcosm of the body of man. (James I's speech to parliament, 21 March, 1610; quoted in Hughes, 1980, p.28)

There was nothing particularly innovative about these ideas, Christian beliefs and the state of society determined that:

> Patriarchal doctrines can be found throughout the Stuart period and in all strata of thought, from well-ordered ... theories, through the ... polemics of tractarians and controversialists to the unstated prejudices of the inarticulate masses. (Schochet, 1975, p.5)

Charles I was not as given to abstract thought as his father had been, but his policies from 1625 to 1642 made it clear that he had inherited his most optimistic interpretation of the royal plenitude of power.

Exercise   Read Coward, pp.151–66 and *Anthology,* III.18. Did Charles recognize any limitation of his royal prerogative?

Discussion   Although Charles 'confessed' that he was parliament's 'instrument' in declaring war on Spain, he went on to make it clear that he could change this policy if he wished. Its continuation was dependant on parliament's submissive co-operation. Failure to please him would lead to their summary dissolution; he conceded no limitation of his prerogative.

During the 1630s it looked as if Charles I might succeed in enforcing the views aired in 1626. Sufficient numbers of his influential subjects were prepared to support him: in terms reminiscent of de Balzac, several judges agreed to his levy of ship money. Their grounds were that, if the safety of the realm was at stake, the king's power was not limited ' ... by rules of law or the property rights of subjects' (Zagorin, 1982, p.144).

Charles I was deeply religious and the extreme claims he made for the extent of his prerogative were derived from the same scripturally based patriarchalism that James had voiced in his 1610 speech. Sir Robert Filmer, an ardent supporter of unlimited royal power, wrote a defence of it in the *Patriarcha* before the outbreak of the civil war. His argument, although deriving much of its authority from the Old Testament, was also strongly influenced by Bodin's concept of the absolute sovereignty of kings. It had little impact at the time as it was not published for another forty years. Yet it stated a case which was to be taken as the definitive Royalist/Tory position by parliamentarians, republicans and Whigs throughout the following century.

Please now read the extract in the *Anthology,* III.19.

Women and political ideas

The *Patriarcha* proposed an ideal image of unquestioned family and state authority exercised by fathers and kings. This had been instituted by the God of the Old Testament in his creation of Adam, to whom he gave rule over the earth and all its creatures including his wife, Eve. By the middle of the century there were plenty of men and women, French peasants, Scottish burghers and their wives, as well as members of the educated élite, who dissented from the patriarchal justification for the unrestrained use of the royal prerogative. But what of these women? Did they hold any views on these matters which could be distinguished from those of the male members of their families?

The two major issues which brought monarchs and their subjects to blows in France and the British Isles were religion and taxation and in these areas women were as concerned as their husbands to seek concessions. Anne Temple, for example, proclaimed in 1640:

> Wee shall see idolatry and superstition rooted out and God's ordinances set up in the puritie and power of them. (Coward, p.189)

Lucy Hutchinson remarked on the duplicity of Charles I:

> ... yet the parliament showed such a wonderful respect to the king, that they never mentioned him, as he was the sole author of all those miscarriages, but imputed them to evil counsellors, and gave him all the submissive language that could have been used to a good prince ... (Hutchinson, 1968, p.75)

Women as well as men rioted against the *gabelle* in France, suffered religious repression in Ireland, were supporters of the Covenant in Scotland and insurgent petitioners in London, printed and disseminated seditious literature and read and listened to it. (See, for example, Manning, 1973, pp.178–222.) The dividing line between political ideas and political activism is hard to distinguish.

No realistic claim can be made that British women were original political thinkers: the arguments which defended or attacked the royal exercise of power were exclusively developed by men although women were actively involved in furthering those policies. Intimations of a new political perspective, pioneered by women who made a case for a role in public life, especially in education, were apparent by the middle of the century:

> ... by an Opinion, which I hope is but an Erroneous one in Men, we are Shut out of all Power and Authority, by reason we are never Employed either in Civil or Martial Affairs, our Counsels are Despised, and Laughed at, the best of our Actions are Trodden down with Scorn, by the Over-weening conceit, Men have of Themselves, and through a Despisement of Us. (Margaret Cavendish, duchess of Newcastle, *Philosophical and Physical Opinions*, 1663; quoted in Perry, 1986, p.115)

The duchess was ridiculed as 'mad Madge', she does seem to have behaved eccentrically, but was her reputation formed partly as a male defensive reaction to her audacious ideas?

Mary Astell enjoyed a high reputation with men and women as a scholarly writer. Many of her works concentrated on religion but *A Serious Proposal to the Ladies*, a seemingly modest suggestion for the establishment of a kind of Protestant nunnery to promote learning for women, could have posed a challenge to male hegemony in higher education (*Anthology*, III.20). Now turn the audio-cassette (AC2, Section 5) to work on the exercise on Mary Astell.

In France there were noble women who were intellectually active – intervening, when they could, in politics, and holding *salons* (see Unit 6, pp.19–26). Yet there is little evidence to indicate that they aspired to challenge male dominance over politics and education.

Madame de Maintenon, who wished for a more modern, secular education for women, did not envisage an independent role for them in society. They were to be brought up as passive and obedient to the male authorities, including their future husbands (see *Anthology*, II.1 (A)–(C)).

The problem of political authority

Unit 3 discussed how France and the British Isles were engulfed in civil conflict during the middle years of the seventeenth century. In the first part of this unit some of the ideas which justified or opposed the nature of the royal governments have been considered. We will now review them, paying particular attention to how events affected the development of ideas about the balance of power between the kings and their subjects.

Exercise   Read Coward, pp.197–204 and Briggs, pp.132–40.

1   In what form were the ideas which encouraged defiance of royal authority expressed?

2   Did the monarchies develop theories to counter the right of resistance claimed by their opponents?

Discussion   1   The English debates in parliament were recorded fairly fully and the numerous petitions, which were presented at this period, often included ideas about how affairs could be re-ordered to achieve the redress of grievances. Similarly in France the transactions of the sovereign courts encapsulated many of the more moderate objections to the perceived misgovernment of the Regency. The nobility prepared some lists of grievances (*cahiers de doléances*) for a meeting of the Estates-General which they hoped would take place during the Fronde. The pamphlets which made personal attacks on Cardinal Mazarin (*Mazarinades*) often included more general ideas about the remedies for his misgovernment.

2   As Coward (p.201) observes, the growing extremism of Pym and his fellows enabled Charles I to pose as the defender of the fundamental laws of the kingdom. He could claim that he was attempting to protect the time-honoured customs and liberties of his subjects

from the encroachments of a power-hungry parliament. He effectively hijacked the arguments from precedent which critics of the Stuarts, such as Sir Edward Coke, had used against them in the early decades of the century. Mazarin, acting on behalf of the young Louis XIV, resorted to no such theoretical justifications. The opposition was disunited and mainly conservative. All he had to do was play off one faction against another and wait for Condé to demonstrate his unreliability as a leader.

The Frondes

Exercise   Read *Anthology*, II.3.

1   Did the conditions laid down in the marriage contract constitute a radical political programme?

2   Did the author pay any regard to provincial interests?

3   Would the conditions laid down in the extract permanently have limited royal power?

Discussion   1   The first four conditions were very conservative, dealing with religious orthodoxy and the protection of the king and his realm. The concern for the welfare of the poor people to be secured 'as far as possible' echoed the sentiments of de Morgues discussed on p.65, above. The other six conditions engaged with the particular grievance of the dominance of Mazarin over the king and the Queen Mother. The demand that the young king should be educated to acquire the necessary virtues was traditional but the requirement that the *parlement* should decide who should be his tutors was a daring innovation striking directly at the absolute sovereignty of the monarchy. The provisions by which counsellors and ministers should be controlled and disciplined were the logical sequel. The differing nature of the conditions demonstrates a major problem for the Frondeurs. They were unable to break away from traditional concepts of government to design a programme which would systematically have limited royal power. They addressed particular grievances with radical solutions which could only alienate the moderates who might have been attracted by a coherent agenda for reform.

2   In the preamble to the conditions for the marriage contract the sisters and brothers of Paris and the *parlement* were mentioned. The former were the other cities of France and the latter the regional *parlements*. This was an attempt to associate provincial movements of discontent as closely as possible with the Frondes in Paris.

3   Although the most spectacular condition was the exemplary execution of Mazarin, there was no indication that, if it had been achieved, the *parlement* would have resumed its former subordinate

LE SALVT DE LA FRANCE,
DANS LES ARMES DE LA VILLE DE PARIS.

A Le bon Genie de la France, conduisant sa Maiesté en sa flotte Royale.
B Son Altesse le Prince de Conty, Generalissime de l'armée du Roy, tenant le timon du Vaisseau, accompagné des Ducs d'Elbeuf, & de Beaufort, Generaux de l'armée, & du Prince de Marsillac, Lieutenant general de l'armée.
C Les Ducs de Boüillon & de la Motte-Haudancour, Generaux, accompagnez du Marquis de Noirmontier, Lieutenant General de l'armée.
D Le Corps du Parlement, accompagné de Messieurs de Ville.
E Le Mazarin, accompagné de ses Monopoleurs, s'efforçant de renuerser la Barque Françoise, par des vents contraires à sa prosperité.
F Le Marquis d'Ancre se noyant, en taschant de couler le Vaisseau à fond, faisant signe au Mazarin de luy prester la main dans sa premiere entreprise.

A fatale reuolution de l'Empire des Troyens sembleroit nous rendre hereditaire de son mal-heur, ainsi que cette Ville retient encore le nom d'vn de ses derniers Princes; si dans la consternation publique de cette maladie generale de l'Estat, Paris, le chef de ce grand corps de la Monarchie Françoise, si redoutable à tous ses ennemis, & qui ne peut estre atterré que par sa propre pesanteur. Si Paris ne s'estoit le premier armé pour la deffense de cette Couronne, & la conseruation de son authorité: les armes de Paris, cette Nef plus renommée que celle d'Argos, sous la conduitte d'vn autre Iason, digne sang de nos Roys, assisté des Polux & des Castor, autres illustres Argonottes, dont l'experience & la valeur nous promettent desia vn port asseuré en commançant à desplier les voiles. Inuincibles Herauts, que l'obiet du peril ne peut arrester; vous n'auez qu'à combattre en cette celebre conqueste qu'vn Dragon, gardien de tous les thresors de la France, vne harpie orgueilleuse des despoüilles & des richesses de ce florissant Royaume, vn serpent qui se r'emplit depuis tant d'années du sang des peuples, & que nostre foiblesse laisse laschement sacrifier tous les iours à son insatiable conuoitise, à la honte de l'Estat, au desauantage de nostre ieune Monarque, & au mespris des Loix & de la Iustice; & qu'apresent tant de sages Nestors s'efforcent de faire reuiure aux despens de leurs propres vies & de tous leurs biens. Mais le mal est si grand & si present, que l'effet du remede consiste à la diligence. Portons donc nos armes vers cet ennemy commun de tous les Estats; & tandis que nostre Prelat assisté de son Clergé porte les bras vers le Ciel comme vn autre Moise, combattons en vrais Iosuez, & autant armés de foy que de fer, croyons nostre victoire certaine, & que Paris meritera de porter vn iour le nom de deffenseur de L'ESTAT & du salut de la FRANCE.

Figure 16
Le Salut de la France dans les Armes de la ville de Paris – popular print on the start of the blockade. *Bibliothèque Mazarine, Paris, Mazarine M15159. Photo: Jean-Loup Charmet.*

position. The condition that the *parlement* should nominate the administrations of the towns surrounding Paris and control their fortifications, combined with the request that the king should return to his capital, looked like an attempt to supervise him. Despite the traditional nature of some of the conditions in the 'Contract', overall it represented an attempt to limit the power of the crown which was similar in kind to the more successful policies pursued by the English parliament a few years earlier.

The ideologies of the English revolution

Political ideas in England during the conflicts of the 1640s and 1650s, in a country which accommodated a successful revolution, achieved more coherence than was the case with any of the Frondeur demands in France. During the early years of the conflict the main point at issue was how much sovereignty the king was prepared to cede to parliament. Moderate pamphleteers such as Philip Hunton and Henry Parker wished to give parliament sufficient power to safeguard the liberties of subjects. By 1642 Parker had developed a contractual theory to justify resistance to royal tyranny:

> Power is originally inherent in the people, and it is nothing else than that might and vigour which ... a society of men contains within itself; and when by ... a law of common consent and agreement, it is derived into such and such hands, God confirms that law ... (Henry Parker, 'Observations upon some of his Majesties late Answers and Expresses'; quoted in Hughes, 1980, p.99)

Theory soon became practice as the Long Parliament attempted to extract from Charles a settlement which would guarantee the continuation of the shared sovereignty they had effectively enjoyed since they were convened. The preamble to the Nineteen Propositions of June, 1642, hoped that he would be:

> ... pleased to grant and accept these their humble desires and propositions as the most necessary effectual means, through God's blessings, of removing those jealousies and differences which have unhappily fallen betwixt you and your people, and procuring both your Majesty and them a constant course of honour, peace and happiness. (Gardiner, 1962, p.250)

The draconian limitations placed on royal power which followed, predicated on the need to remove those 'differences' between Charles and his subjects, made it clear who was being blamed for the situation. The 'peace and happiness' of his subjects was valued as highly as the king's own and could only be secured by curtailing his prerogative.

The victory of parliament in the ensuing civil wars did not advance their political thinking concerning a new basis for the exercise of authority. Until 1647 kingship was generally perceived as a constitutional necessity and then it was only a minority of radicals, such as the Levellers in London and the army, who demanded an alternative.

Exercise   Read *Anthology*, III.21 and Coward, pp.228–33.
In the first *Agreement of the People* (*Anthology*, III.21) how much power was to be vested in parliament?

Discussion   The king was only referred to once, in a very hostile fashion, at the end of the document. A reformed parliament, with rationalized constituencies, was to take over many of his powers. It would make laws, appoint to all public offices, make war and peace and conclude treaties with foreign powers. Important rights were reserved to individuals: real equality before the law and religious toleration were to be part of the new order.

    Now turn on the audio-cassette (AC2, Section 5) and do the exercise on the Putney Debates (*Anthology*, I.18).
The execution of Charles I in 1649 was justified by the court which had been set up to try him on the grounds that he had abused the power entrusted to him and by the rights:

> … which by the fundamental constitutions of this kingdom were reserved on the peoples' behalf in the right and power of frequent and successive Parliaments. (Sentence of the High Court of Justice upon the King, January 27, 1649; in Gardiner, 1962, p.377)

The Rump and army grandees, who had finally resolved to be rid of the king, wished to tie their case firmly to the traditional rights and liberties of Englishmen. Reversion to the arguments invoked in the early years of the century avoided the danger of reviving the case made by the Levellers for greater political participation by the common people. No mention was made of any contract either originally made between king and people or violated by Charles I.
The problem with all appeals to precedent and fundamental law as justification for a new, republican form of government, was that they came up against the question Charles I had asked at his trial. By what authority could any new institution be created? Ironically the most satisfactory answer to this question came from a royalist rather than a republican.

Exercise   Read Offprint 18, Coward, pp.238–44 and *Anthology*, III.22.

1   What features of Thomas Hobbes's political ideas could reconcile Englishmen to the overthrow of the monarchy?

2   What was so revolutionary about Gerrard Winstanley's approach to authority?

3   Distinguish between the kinds of republicanism which were advocated during the Commonwealth.

Discussion   1   Hobbes in the *Leviathan* envisaged an original state of anarchy in which individuals warred against each other. To avoid this peoples made contracts amongst themselves to surrender their independence to a sovereign who would have absolute power. This sovereign, or 'Leviathan', could be a king, a group of lords or a popular

Figure 17
Title-page of Thomas
Hobbes's, Leviathan...,
1651, Mansell Collection.

assembly. The right to exercise absolute power depended on the ability to protect the people. The overthrow of the sovereign absolved subjects from the obligation of obedience which was transferred to the victor. Religion played no part in these transactions, the clergy were to be subordinated to the state.

2   Whilst most political thinkers, even Hobbes and the Levellers, started with society as it existed, Winstanley wanted to change it radically. All private ownership of the land and its products would be abolished, sufficient for subsistence would be distributed to all, in return everyone would work for the common good. Law and a centralized state would be made redundant by universal education but, as a transitional measure, magistrates would oversee the institution of the new order. The rejection of property and privilege and the fact that he tried to put his ideas into operation by digging up St George's Hill near Weybridge in Surrey, caused Winstanley and his Diggers to be regarded as dangerous subversives by almost all shades of opinion.

3   Cromwell and his associates were *de facto* republicans once the king had been executed. This was from expediency rather than conviction, however, and they did not formulate a rationale for their action. The ancient world provided convenient models of republicanism during the Interregnum, but the most notable was produced by James Harrington in *The Commonwealth of Oceana* (1656). The basis of his republican regime was to be an equitable distribution of property. A senate, an assembly and a state church would exercise secular and spiritual authority.

The republican ideas which flourished during the Interregnum continued to influence politicians like Algernon Sidney and Anthony Ashley Cooper (Lord Shaftesbury) after the Restoration. They mounted an uncompromising opposition to Charles II's absolutist policies which culminated in plotting rebellion. This republican tradition influenced the thought of John Locke and his writings before and after the Revolution of 1688. The Frondes, which had not produced any coherent alternative to unlimited kingly power, left no such intellectual legacy to potential opponents of absolutism.

France 1661–1715: the absolutism of Louis XIV and its critics
(Antony Lentin)

In this part of the unit we shall be looking at a selection of primary sources, by contemporary French commentators of varying background, relating to Louis XIV, his person and policies. By examining these sources, you can build up a picture of ways in which Louis's rule was seen at the time by himself and others, and how far (if at all) there developed a critical counter-ideology in France, comparable to those in England.

Louis XIV

Exercise   Read *Anthology*, III.23 (A).

1   How reliable do you consider it to be as evidence of Louis's views on monarchical authority, and why?

2   What does it tell us of those views?

3   How does Louis justify his claims?

Discussion 1   As part of a confidential document intended for the use and guidance of his son and heir by a king desirous to pass on his recent
experience, it can be relied on as a sincere expression of Louis's
belief in monarchy and the principles underlying it.

2   With the recent traumatic events of the Frondes certainly in mind,
Louis vigorously asserts three basic principles of government. First,
the divine right of kings, who rule as God's representatives on earth.
Second, their right to rule absolutely, being accountable for their
actions only to God. Third, and most important, the corresponding
duty of unconditional obedience to the ruler by his subjects. This
excerpt is a trenchant statement of the principle of divine-right
monarchy.

3   All three assertions are based first and foremost on biblical precept
(e.g. St Paul in Romans 13). The duty of passive obedience is
described as 'this law, so express and so universal' and as the most
'firmly established' of Christian principles. It is also justified on
utilitarian grounds as 'salutary' for the people and in any case far
preferable to the dangerous alternative of resistance.

Exercise   Now read *Anthology*, III.23 (B). Summarize what it tells us about Louis's
policy towards the Huguenots.

Discussion   The extract, written a dozen years before Louis's revocation of the Edict
of Nantes (1685), provides startling evidence of his long-term intention
to eliminate Protestantism altogether and restore uniformity of religion
in France. As a Catholic monarch, Louis regards the Huguenots as her-
etics ('these pernicious errors'), and his objections to Protestantism seem
to be on religious grounds alone, since he encourages their conversion to
Catholicism. For the present, he proposes not to repeal their existing
privileges under the Edict of Nantes. These will, however, be interpreted
restrictively. At the same time, he will encourage the Huguenots to return
to the dominant faith by financial inducements and by activating the
Catholic clergy to evangelize. He strongly hints, however, that he has further measures in mind, to be enacted at some future time. (What were
these? See Briggs, p.153 and *Anthology*, III.9.)

Exercise   What does *Anthology*, III.23 (C) suggest about Louis and his attitude to
war and how reliable do you consider it as evidence of this attitude?

Discussion   The overriding impression is of Louis's immense and continual concern
for his image and reputation as king of France, and his association of the
'good of the state' with his own 'grandeur and pride'. He protests, no
doubt sincerely, his desire for peace in the last years of his reign; but what
shows through is pride in the overall achievements of his foreign policy
and repugnance at the notion of submitting to humiliating conditions 'at
the cost of my reputation or at least of my personal satisfaction and perhaps of my glory'. In Louis's conception, war itself reflects the prestige of
the state ('the grandeur and pride befitting this realm') and has in his
reign brought about territorial expansion and a secure (eastern) frontier.
The king's duty is to work for a victorious or at least an honourable con-

clusion, consistent with his own prestige ('my reputation', 'my glory'). As a draft proclamation, designed to rally public support at a bad time, the document contains what Louis wanted the people to believe; but in its defence of his foreign policy, it also reflects his deepest convictions about his own role as a monarch. Briggs (p.149) describes Louis's foreign policy as 'the pursuit of glory' and refers to 'an obsessive concern for the prestige of his dynasty' (p.150).

Bossuet

Exercise Read *Anthology*, III.24 (A) and (B).

1 Do you detect significant similarities between Bossuet's approach and that of Louis in *Anthology*, III.23?

2 Do you think there are important differences between them?

3 Do you detect any significant difference of emphasis in Bossuet's two documents, which were written fifty years apart?

Discussion 1 Like Louis, Bossuet upholds the theory of divine-right monarchy based on scriptural authority: the king rules by divine right as God's representative. (Bossuet actually asserts that 'a divine element attaches to the prince'.) Like Louis, he also claims that divine right monarchy exists 'for the good of mankind'.

2 As a churchman, Bossuet quotes precise biblical authority, where Louis simply refers generally to Scripture. However, while Louis insists on the absolute authority of kings and the subjects' duty of 'humble submission', Bossuet stresses the king's corresponding duty, also laid on him by Scripture, to rule 'in accordance with his [God's] laws', that is, compassionately, even under the strains of war. Bossuet hints, tactfully but explicitly, that Louis's taxation policy is too harsh. While Louis demands unconditional obedience, therefore, Bossuet also indicates that the king is not above reproof, at any rate from the clergy.

3 Fifty years after his letter to Louis, Bossuet advances the same divine-right argument (Scripture says 'Ye are Gods'). As in *Anthology*, III.24 (A), however, he qualifies this by reminding the king that as a human being ('gods of flesh and blood') he is also mortal.

Figure 18
Jacques Bénigne Bossuet (1627–1704), *portrait by Hyacinthe Rigaud (1659–1743). Musée du Louvre. Photo: Lauros-Giraudon.*

The strong emotive tone of Bossuet's language indicates that even the most eloquent supporters of divine-right monarchy believed that the king, though not accountable to his subjects, was bound to rule mercifully as a Christian king.

As Mettam (1990, p.50) observes, 'even Bossuet, often cited as the panegyrist of divine-right absolutism, tempered his enthusiasm for powerful monarchy with some severe moral strictures'.

La Bruyère

Exercise   Read *Anthology*, III.25 (A)–(D), and briefly note the subject matter of each. What, in each case, do you take to be La Bruyère's attitude to monarchy in France?

Discussion *Extract (A)*
As the title of the section makes clear, the subject matter is the court. La Bruyère's attitude is critical and cynical. Life at Versailles is trivial but all-engaging, and morally corrupt: 'Vice and politeness have equal sway'.
Extract (B)
Here, thinly disguised as part of a purported account of some strange and exotic country, is an account of religious observance in the royal chapel at Versailles. By describing it with ironic detachment, La Bruyère brings out the worldliness of the court, whose concerns are remote from religion or the moral principles urged by Bossuet in *Anthology*, III.24 (and preached by him at Versailles).
Extract (C)
Here, La Bruyère gives a picture of the bloodshed caused by Louis's wars. His expression of regret for the loss of the two Soyecourt brothers (La Bruyère was a friend of the family) killed at the battle of Fleurus in 1690, reminds the reader of the serious side to the author's satire. The generalization on war, on the other hand, is mordantly thought-provoking: La Bruyère makes war seem absurd as well as cruel and unjust, and by implication he criticizes Louis's campaigns for territorial expansion as aggressive and unnecessary, where Bossuet (*Anthology*, III.24 (A)) suggests that they are wars of defence.
Extract (D)
The subject matter is political theory: the extent of the mutual duties of monarch and subject. La Bruyère holds that even absolute rulers have duties ('indispensable obligations') and should rule paternally: they are in a sense accountable, or at least their claims to particular prerogatives are open to debate. He denies the claim (asserted by Louis in his *Mémoires*) to be 'absolute master' of his subjects' goods. The implication of his allegory of the sheep and the shepherd – 'Was the flock made for the shepherd or the shepherd for the flock?' – is made explicit by La Bruyère. He continues the metaphor to criticize 'a gorgeous and sumptuous monarch', that is, Louis and the extravagance of Versailles.

Figure 19
Jean de la Bruyère in 1693, *painting by Elisabeth Vigée-Lebrun (1755–1842). Musée National du Château de Versailles Inv. MV.2940. Photo: Giraudon.*

Exercise   Think again about the extracts you have just read. Do you detect any important respect in which La Bruyère's attitude towards Louis XIV differs from Bossuet's?

Discussion La Bruyère's tone as a satirist is obviously sharper than Bossuet's. As a moralist, however, his plea for milder rule in *Anthology*, III.25 (D) parallels Bossuet's. He goes further than Bossuet in detailing those aspects of Louis's rule of which he disapproves. He does not, like Bossuet, relate absolute rule to divine right or biblical authority; indeed he suggests that absolutism has its limits, though avowedly he does not spell them out (apart from denying Louis's claim to be 'absolute master of all his subjects' goods'). On the other hand, he does not appear to question monarchy as an institution.

Saint-Simon

Exercise   Read *Anthology*, III.26 (A)–(D).

1   Note briefly the subject matter of each extract.

2   Comment on any particular bias you may detect.

Discussion   1   In extract (A) Saint-Simon gives an account of Louis's character, contrasting his natural charm with his desire 'to reign by himself', his alleged 'vanity' and 'love of glory', to which is attributed his aggressive foreign policy.

Extract (B) instances Louis's grace and politeness, his love of magnificence and extravagance, his choice of Versailles and Marly.

Extract (C) describes the effects of the revocation of the Edict of Nantes and Louis's reaction to it.

Extract (D) describes Louis's 'manner of living when with the army'.

2   Although Saint-Simon is our main primary source on Louis at Versailles, he clearly held strong and hostile views, which should be studied with caution.

In *Anthology*, III.26 (A), while conceding that Louis would have excelled in living the private life of 'a simple private gentleman' (a somewhat backhanded compliment) and even that he was 'by disposition good and just', Saint-Simon claims that Louis's basic urge was his 'vanity' and his desire to rule alone. This, though obviously hostile, sounds fair comment (to judge, for example, from Louis's own words in *Anthology*, III.23 (C)). He goes on to claim that because of his own defective education (his intellect was 'beneath mediocrity'), Louis deliberately chose ministers inferior to himself. Louis's alleged ignorance should be queried: does the evidence of his own writings (*Anthology*, III.23) bear it out?

In *Anthology*, III.26 (B), he details Louis's exquisite courtesy and politeness. But his account of his graded forms of salutation perhaps suggests a criticism of Louis's concern with minutiae, his interest 'in little things' asserted in III.26 (A). Saint-Simon deplores the power enjoyed by Louis's valets, and the alleged fact that even ministers and princes of the blood sought their favour. To Saint-Simon, a duke himself, this was a disgrace. He sounds the same note of aristocratic disdain and disapproval in criticizing the spread of luxury across society, particularly the resulting 'general confusion of rank'. His complaints extend to Louis's love of buildings: to Saint-Simon the buildings, especially at Versailles, demonstrate 'pride', 'caprice' and 'bad taste'. (You can judge this for yourself on the evidence of TV1). More significantly, he deplores their cost, complaining of 'a palace so immense and so immensely dear', while 'Versailles, even, did not cost so much as Marly'.

Figure 20
*Pierre Denis Martin le Jeune
(1663–1742),* Bassin
d'Apollon and Grand
Canal, Versailles. *Musée
National du Château de
Versailles – Grand Trianon
Inv. MV. 757. Photo:
Giraudon.*

Statistics bear out this claim: the cost of building Versailles rose from 5 million livres in 1679 to over 11 million in 1685; the cost of building Marly was about 4 million. The cost of refurbishing the palace of Saint-Germain was about 6 million (Wolf, 1968, p.358).

In *Anthology*, III.26 (C), Saint-Simon shows total hostility to Louis's policy against the Huguenots after 1685, attributing it partly to the influence of Mme de Maintenon (this claim is denied by modern historians, see Wolf, 1968, p.335); and more particularly to Louis's 'profound ignorance' and bigotry – 'he was devout with the grossest ignorance'. Given his underlying vanity, this made him 'an easy prey to the Jesuits'; credulous and gullible – 'The monarch doubted not of the sincerity of this crowd of conversions'.

We may also conclude from this extract, if Saint-Simon's account is to be believed, that Louis's policy did not command universal approval, even among the Catholic majority. He claims that it was deplored by 'the good and true Catholics and the true bishops' (cf. Fénelon, bishop of Cambrai, below). Briggs, however (p.153), sums up the consensus among modern historians, in stating that Louis's policy enjoyed 'enormous popularity... among Catholic Frenchmen at the time'.

In *Anthology*, III.26 (D), he complains that except 'when with the army', he 'never ate with any man'. The nobility as a whole, with rare exceptions, was excluded from the king's table, since 'the number of the persons from whom a choice was made was very limited'.

This complaint is borne out by the known facts. Out of some 100,000 men, women and children who counted as 'people of quality' in France, no more than 250 individuals 'had the right to live in more or less easy intercourse with the king'. (Wolf, 1968, p.273).

Saint-Simon was born into the highest and most ancient nobility. His father received his dukedom from Louis XIII, and Saint-Simon was particularly sensitive to slights on his rank: peers and dukes ranked after the princes of the blood and nobles whose families ruled abroad. As a courtier at Versailles, Saint-Simon had the opportunity to observe what he described (albeit long afterwards) in his *Memoirs*, but his accounts are highly coloured by long pent-up spleen and hostility, particularly in his attitude to Louis's character and policies. Believing that the role of the nobility should be that of a ruling caste, he resented the largely decorative role at court to which Louis reduced them after the Fronde. He deplored what he saw as the rise of non-nobles on whom Louis depended for the establishment of his absolute monarchy. (Historians have shown this view of Louis's raising up a 'vile bourgeoisie' to be much exaggerated.) Moreover Saint-Simon had political ambitions of his own: he attached himself to the Duke of Burgundy (whom he extols in his *Memoirs*), looking forward to his accession in order to promote his own fortunes; and when Burgundy died in 1712, he became a supporter of the Duke of Orléans, a member of the Regency Council on Louis's death in 1715, and later ambassador to Spain.

Exercise What conclusions do you draw from the *Memoirs* about Saint-Simon's attitude to monarchy?

Discussion Like La Bruyère, Saint-Simon does not appear to believe in the divine right of kings, not at any rate in the sense (which Louis and Bossuet adhered to) that kings were above criticism by their subjects, since he judges and harshly criticizes Louis's person and policy throughout the reign. On the other hand, he admits that in spite of everything, Louis had enough natural gifts 'to enable him to be a good king', and there is no clear indication in the present extracts that he favoured any system of government other than absolute monarchy.

Bayle

Exercise   Read *Anthology*, III.27. What is Bayle's approach to Louis's policy towards the Huguenots?

Discussion   Bayle is utterly opposed to Louis's policy: 'Nothing is more abominable than to make conversions by force'. From what we know of Bayle and his personal experience as a Huguenot, this comes as no surprise. (His brother, a pastor, died in prison in 1686 as the result of attempts by Catholics to force him to convert.) As a Protestant, Bayle is obviously anti-Catholic in his explicit attempt to counter the arguments drawn from the Bible by supporters of Louis's policy such as Bossuet. While declining to explain what the passage in St Luke might mean, he is adamant in 'refuting the literal meaning which the persecutors give to it'. He reaches his conclusion by way of the Protestant tradition of bringing reason and conscience to bear on questions of scriptural interpretation. This leads to the conclusion that 'any literal meaning which entails the obligation to commit crimes is false'. He contrasts this approach with the Catholic argument (favoured, notably, by Bossuet) based on unquestioning submission to the authority of the church and the church Fathers.

Exercise   In *Anthology*, III.26 (C), you will recall Saint-Simon's discussion of the revocation of the Edict of Nantes. Re-read that extract and compare it with that of Bayle.

1   Do you find any significant *similarities* in the attitude of the two writers towards Louis's policy on the Huguenots?

2   Do you find any significant *differences* in the attitude of the two writers towards Louis's policy on the Huguenots?

Discussion   1   Both writers, Catholic and Protestant, show a common horror and outrage. Both complain in similar terms, of the brutality and futility of Louis's policy (including the hypocrisy of forced conversions – 'simulated abjuration' says Saint-Simon), and its inconsistency with France's true interests, political and economic.

2   Saint-Simon's account (as was noted earlier) takes the form of a highly personalized attack on Louis, attributing royal policy to his vanity. Bayle's account, by contrast, takes the form of an analytical critique of the policy itself and the reasoning behind it. Bayle's object is not merely to denounce that policy but to explain why it is illogical and self-defeating, why 'this use of constraint to establish a religion is false', and why Christ's words cannot properly be used to justify it. The policy is 'in evident contradiction with common sense'. While Saint-Simon simply denounces persecution, Bayle argues that religious pluralism and toleration (which Louis's supporters considered a 'dangerous plague in a state'), would bring immense benefits to France

Bayle's religious pluralism, his appeal to common sense and his critical approach to Scripture were felt, even outside France, to verge on scepticism, particularly with the appearance of his *Historical and Critical Dictionary* (1695–7: see Briggs, p.195 and Unit 6, p.31). Briggs (p.164) claims that Bayle's 'sceptical writings constituted a subtle but deadly assault on the values by which the king had lived'. They had a powerful influence on the moral and philosophical reaction against those values in the eighteenth century, known as the Enlightenment (which are a focus of the course A206 *The Enlightenment*).

Fénelon

Exercise   Read *Anthology*, III.28 and briefly summarize its complaints. Note any examples of bias that strike you.

Discussion   1   The passage is a sustained attack on Louis's foreign policy as aggressive. Inspired by his love of 'glory', this policy has alienated all the neighbouring states. Like La Bruyère and Saint-Simon, Fénelon claims that Louis's policy since 1672 has led only to more wars. The peace treaties of 1672–94 have only been truces. (Briggs, pp.151–6, broadly agrees with this interpretation.)

2   Even in peace-time, Louis has pursued a policy of creeping expansion in Alsace through the *Chambres de réunion*. (See Briggs, p.230, *Réunions.*)

3   The strains imposed by Louis's foreign policy have led to agricultural and economic depression and social unrest.

4   Blinded by flattery and self-regard, Louis ignores the reality of France's sufferings. God will humiliate him; for Louis's religion lacks true unction.

Exercise   How, briefly, would you describe Fénelon's attitude as compared with that of other commentators?

Discussion   Though the language is more outspoken, the sentiments expressed are shared by La Bruyère, Saint-Simon and even by Bossuet.

Briggs (p.163) states that Fénelon 'appreciated the extent of the miseries Louis had brought on his people'. Louis's biographer, J.B. Wolf (1968, p.73), on the other hand, argues that Fénelon wrote 'rather smugly' and refers to Fénelon's 'pious, lofty and somewhat impractical idealism'. Another of Louis's biographers, F. Bluche (1990, p.455), complains of 'bad faith': Fénelon, he argues, ignored Louis's strenuous efforts to relieve food shortages during the harsh winters of 1693 and 1694, and elevated temporary bread riots into significant uprisings (which they were not).

Exercise   Think about the extracts you have just read and use them as a basis for answering the following questions.

1   How *reliable* do you consider the criticisms of French absolutism?

2   How *radical* do you consider the criticisms of French absolutism?

Discussion 1 Bossuet, La Bruyère, Saint-Simon, Bayle and Fénelon were well-known public figures and highly articulate writers. Their writings are the products of an educational and social élite. All but Bayle were able to observe Louis at first hand, and Bayle suffered personally from Louis's policy. All are outspoken in criticizing aspects of Louis's rule, particularly in the second half of the reign, notably the luxury of Versailles, foreign policy and the sufferings of the people. Even allowing for extreme bias in Saint-Simon, *Anthology*, III.24–28 suggest a common discontent with aspects of Louis's rule and a close consensus on the areas of French life where its effects were most harmful.

2 Internal criticism of Louis remained covert (in Briggs's words 'oblique and qualified', p.195). Saint-Simon and Fénelon were kept under surveillance. Apart from Bayle, a refugee in Holland, only La Bruyère ventured to publish his criticisms in his lifetime, and these, though extremely outspoken, were presented in a literary guise. Other than Bayle, only Saint-Simon (who wrote in the eighteenth century) censures Louis's suppression of the Huguenots (and both La Bruyère and Fénelon state elsewhere that they regard the enforcement of religious uniformity as part of the king's duty).

Figure 21
François de Salignac de la Mothe-Fénelon (1651–1715), *portrait by Joseph Vivien (1657–1734). Musée National du Château de Versailles. Photo: Bulloz.*

There is no evidence of opposition to absolutism as such, no reference to social contract theory (except in La Bruyère), or to a constitutional form of monarchy on the English model of 1689. Republicanism found some support among the Huguenots; but all four writers (including Bayle, see Briggs, p.195) supported absolute monarchy as such, and Bossuet's severe and outspoken moral strictures as Louis's spiritual adviser are perfectly consistent with the kind of absolutism, accountable only to God and the moral law, which Bodin had argued for in the preceding century. Saint-Simon and Fénelon, as tutors to the heirs apparent, also hoped to influence policy but not radically to alter the institutional or ideological basis of monarchy. None projected an alternative system of government. As Mettam (1990, p.51) says; 'hardly a voice was raised against monarchy as a system of government in seventeenth-century France – not least because there was no obvious alternative to it'. Note Briggs's description of Saint-Simon and Fénelon as 'aristocratic critics' and his dismissal of 'the reactionary and impractical nature' of their ideas for reform (p.163). There were no equivalents to Locke or Halifax in the France of Louis XIV.

Exercise For a document on Louis and his absolutism from lower down the social scale, read the account written immediately after Louis's death by the parish priest from Saint-Sulpice, near Blois (quoted by Briggs, pp.164–5). Does this document corroborate or add anything new to the evidence of the documents you have studied in this section?

Discussion The priest's account testifies to the immediate appearance after his death in 1715 of expressions of popular discontent with Louis in the form of verses, songs, sayings, etc. Is the objection to Louis's abuse of absolutism? Or to absolutism itself?

Republicanism in the British Isles

(Lucille Kekewich)

Royalists may have believed that the restoration of the monarchy in 1660 had laid to rest all debate concerning the merits of republicanism. The developments of the next three decades: the question of toleration, the Exclusion Crisis and the Stuarts' pro-French policies, revived enthusiasm for various versions of the 'Good Old Cause'. An Irishman, John Toland, promoted this by publishing the works of James Harrington and contemporary republican writers such as Algernon Sidney.

An effective attack which their opponents could make upon the Stuarts was to question their right to maintain any kind of standing army, always seen as a symbol of absolute monarchy. This was the line taken in pamphlets by the Scot, Andrew Fletcher of Saltoun, and the historian, John Toland. Moderate critics of the royal government could be persuaded to support such an offensive, which was orchestrated through a pamphlet campaign. For republicans such concentration on attempts to limit specific royal powers was to prove more profitable than wholesale assaults on the institution of monarchy.

Exercise   Read *Anthology*, III.29 (A) and (B). What were the main concerns in the extracts?

Discussion   Both passages were concerned with the danger that standing armies would allow their princes to exercise absolute power. In Extract (A) this was succinctly expressed: '… he that is armed, is always master of the purse of him that is unarmed'. In Extract (B) it was stated more obliquely through the title of the pamphlet, that a militia could be efficient without endangering public liberty. A second concern was fear of tyrannical foreign powers. (A) ' … most princes in Europe are in possession of the sword, by standing mercenary armies', (B) 'our free militia … is the best method of waging the wars abroad'. This preoccupation by republicans and royalists alike was understandable in a decade when William III's armies were seen as the only bastion against the aggression of Catholic, absolute powers.

The development of political ideas in Scotland throughout the century had been strongly influenced by two features of national life: the Presbyterian religion of the majority and the union of the crown with that of England in the person of successive Stuart monarchs.

Presbyterian ideology was rooted in the popular history of the Scottish reformation, in Knox and Buchanan's [reforming contemporaries of Mary, Queen of Scots in the previous century] political ideas, and in … [the] advocacy of a separation of church and state. The two kingdom theory, which excluded the king from church affairs while claiming the right of the church to instruct the king on civil matters pertaining to the godliness of the community, was central to royal objections to presbytery. (Brown, 1992, p.77)

Figure 22
Andrew Fletcher of Saltoun, *portrait by unknown painter after William Aikman, oil on canvas, 76.2 cm. x 63.5 cm. Scottish National Portrait Gallery, reproduced by permission of the National Galleries of Scotland.*

The role played by Scotland in the civil wars predisposed many of its prominent Lowland citizens in the later part of the century to Whiggish opinions: the writings of Fletcher of Saltoun demonstrate the tendency to contribute to as well as to reflect their ideology. On the matter of the parliamentary union with England, finalized in 1707, many, including Fletcher, were fearful that the interests of their country would be subordinated to those of England and that their characteristic legal and political institutions, as well as their culture, would be at risk. The predominance of Presbyterianism not only safeguarded the latter but probably also ensured that an identifiable Scottish strand in British intellectual life should survive at least until the early nineteenth century.

In Ireland the Catholic majority had remained loyal to the Stuarts throughout the century. In 1641 they rose in support of Charles I:

> We are in no rebellion ourselves, but do really fight for our Prince in defence of his Crown and royal prerogatives. (Boyce, Eccleshall and Geoghegan, 1993, p.14)

After a brief period under James II, when their political aspirations seemed about to be fulfilled, they relapsed into a long period as second-class citizens. They pinned their essentially royalist, conservative hopes on 'the king over the water'.

As Blair Worden (1991) points out, the main importance of republican thought in Britain, especially that of Harrington, was the impact it had in the next century:

> In exploring the deficiencies of monarchy the republican writers ... addressed a fundamental problem ... of contemporary politics, and gave men an alternative language to those of the more insular tradition of law and precedent ... Classical political language, and the doctrine of the balance, became commonplace in eighteenth century political discussion. (Worden, 1991, pp.474–5)

John Locke

> ... the impressive intellectual contribution made by John Locke to our cultural heritage arose out of the political turmoil that surrounded him as the trusted adviser of the most important opposition politician in Restoration England. (Ashcraft, 1986, p.79)

Ashcraft has taken John Locke, originally an Oxford don, out of his study and shown him to have been Lord Shaftesbury's political agent for many years. After the earl's death, Locke's notoriety as a subversive radical forced him to remain in exile until the accession of William III. Ashcraft claims that he was actively involved in the Rye House plot and in raising finance for Monmouth's Rebellion. Locke's ideas are contained in a number of tracts and treatises which influenced the thinking of the Whigs. His *A Letter Concerning Toleration* (1685), confirmed their view that dissenters should be allowed to practise their religion without breaking the law. The first of *The Two Treatises on Civil Government*, shown by Laslett (1963) to have been written in the early 1680s, was an answer to the large claims for royal authority made in Filmer's *Patriarcha*, which had recently been published. Locke divorced the obligation to respect paternal authority from the question of political obedience. The second part of the work arose out of the debates between the radicals and those who wished to preserve the fullest powers for the monarchy.

Exercise   Read *Anthology*, III.30.

1   What three kinds of power did Locke distinguish?

2   How was the second shown to be superior to the first and third?

3   Do you detect the influence of other seventeenth-century thinkers in Locke's work?

Discussion   1   Paternal power was exercised over children but only until they reached the age of reason. It did not extend over their property or imply any political jurisdiction. Political power came from the compact of all men in a state of nature that they would devolve their individual power onto a society whose representative was a magistrate. In return, their lives, liberties and property were guaranteed by a government which could not be arbitrary or unjust. Despotic power had no foundation in reason or in nature and could legitimately be destroyed by those who suffered from it.

2   Political power was superior to paternal power because it existed permanently whilst it was properly used to protect lives and property. It arose out of a freely made contract and should always be used in accordance with reason. Conversely despotic power was inferior and temporary, grounded neither in nature nor in reason.

3   The discussion of paternal power was a reaction to Filmer with his large claims for a kingly power founded on patriarchalism. Leveller thought of the 1640s probably influenced Locke. He was vague about establishing what classes of men should have full political rights but did refer to: ' ... that power which every man, having in the state of nature ...' The whole idea of men, in a state of nature, agreeing to surrender some of their individual liberty to form a society, owed something to Hobbes. The conclusions which Locke drew were, however, very different from those of the *Leviathan*.

Similarities and contrasts: British and French views of the state

Many parallels may be drawn between the development of political ideas in France and in the British Isles during the early seventeenth century. Both kings sought to justify their claims to extensive powers to suppress religious dissent, wage foreign wars and pay for them by arbitrarily levying taxes. These claims elicited counter-arguments from their subjects,

the *Nu-pieds* and *Croquants* in France, the programmes of parliamentarians like Parker and Hunton in England. During the crisis of the 1640s
and early 1650s the monarchy was overthrown in Britain and seriously
threatened in France. It produced the demands of the Levellers as well as
the equally shocking *Leviathan* of Hobbes, which envisaged a ruler whose
only justification was the ability to impose a sovereign will. In France the
authors of the *Mazarinades* proposed a series of measures which limited
the powers of the existing monarchy, leaving most of its institutions
intact.

The second half of the century saw a divergence in thought between
the two states: in both the emergent aspirations of the common people
and (in England) of a few women to have a political voice were
expressed: in neither were they satisfied. In France however, the energies
of the peasants and bourgeoisie were concentrated on attempting to gain
the redress of particular grievances, in England the new agenda proposed
by the Levellers and their supporters at the end of the civil wars
remained a strand in the political consciousness of the common people.
The British monarchy could never recover the mystique it had claimed
before the civil war. The example of French 'tyranny' encouraged both
survivors from those times and a new generation of theorists like Toland,
Fletcher and Locke to justify the severe curtailment of royal power. Ironically the compromise which emerged after 1688 which allowed a parliament elected on property qualifications to share power with the
monarchy, owed much to the ideas about balance of the republican
writer, James Harrington. The Whigs, who dominated parliament
throughout most of the eighteenth century, preferred to acclaim John
Locke, with his acceptable guarantees of the lives, liberties and status
of property owners, as their ideological authority. In France under Louis
XIV, absolute monarchy was accepted as the only legitimate form of
government. Important writers such as La Bruyère, Saint-Simon or Fénelon never seriously questioned the institution or the extensive powers of
the monarchy, only the way in which the latter had been exercised,
though the seeds of some contemporary criticism were to grow in the
following century.

References

Ashcraft, R. (1986), *Revolutionary Politics and Locke's 'Two Treatises of Government'*, Princeton University Press, Princeton, N.J.

Bluche, F. (1990), *Louis XIV,* translated by M. Greengrass, Basil Blackwell, Oxford.

Boyce, D.G., Eccleshall, R. and Geoghegan, V. (eds) (1993), *Political Thought in Ireland Since the Seventeenth Century,* Routledge, London.

Brown, K.M. (1992), *Kingdom or Province? Scotland and the Regal Union, 1603–1715,* Macmillan, London.

Burns, J.H. and Goldie, M. (eds) (1991), *The Cambridge History of Political Thought, 1450–1700,* Cambridge University Press, Cambridge.

Camden, W. (1610), *Britain or a Chorographicall Description of the most flourishing Kingdoms, England, Scotland and Ireland,* translated into English by Philemon Holland, London.

Church, W.F. (1972), *Richelieu and Reason of State,* Princeton University Press, Princeton, N.J.

Gardiner S.R. (1962) *Constitutional Documents of the Puritan Revolution, 1625–1660,* Clarendon Press, Oxford.

Hughes, A. (ed.) (1980), *Seventeenth-Century England: A Changing Culture I Primary Sources,* Ward Lock, London.

Hutchinson, L. (1968), *Memoirs of the Life of Colonel Hutchinson,* Everyman's Library, London.

Laslett, P. (ed.) (1963), *John Locke: Two Treatises of Government: A Critical Edition,* Cambridge University Press, Cambridge.

Ligou, D. (1968), *Le Protestantisme en France de 1598 à 1715,* Paris.

Manning, B. (ed.) (1973), *Politics, Religion and the English Civil War,* Edward Arnold, London.

Mettam, R. (1990), 'France', in J. Miller (ed.), *Absolutism in Seventeenth-Century Europe* (Problems in Focus series), Macmillan, London.

Perry, R. (1986), *The Celebrated Mary Astell,* University of Chicago Press, Chicago.

Pocock, J.G.A. (1987), *The Ancient Constitution and the Feudal Law,* Cambridge University Press, Cambridge.

Schochet, G.J. (1975), *Patriarchalism in Political Thought: the Authoritarian Family and Political Speculation and Attitudes Especially in Seventeenth Century England,* Basil Blackwell, Oxford.

Skinner, Q. (1978), *The Foundations of Modern Political Thought,* vol.1, Cambridge University Press, Cambridge.

Wolf, J.B. (1968), *Louis XIV,* The History Book Club.

Worden, B. (1991), 'English Republicans', in J.H. Burns and M. Goldie (1991).

Zagorin, P. (1982), *Rebels and Rulers, 1500-1660,* vol.2, Cambridge University Press, Cambridge.

Unit 14
The impact of French culture in Britain

Prepared for the course team by Antony Lentin

Contents

Study timetable

Weeks of study	Texts	Video	AC	Set books
2	*Anthology,* III.31–37; Illustration Book	Video 12	AC2, section 6	

You are also advised to view again TV1 and TV2 to remind yourself of the buildings discussed in the unit. (You should also look again at TV3 and TV4 during the two weeks.)

Objectives
The objectives of the unit are:

1   to assist you in familiarizing yourself with particular aspects of British culture in the period by examining certain selected artefacts and other primary sources;

2   to compare these with similar French examples in order to assess how far and in what ways you feel that French culture was a significant influence in the British Isles in the seventeenth century.

Please note that fulfilling objective 2 will not always be easy. In some cases there is direct evidence of French influence, as when the patron or architect, writer or musician states that they had a French original in mind. In other cases, the evidence is circumstantial: we may infer a French influence from similarities of style which seem too striking to be mere coincidence. But our conclusions both about particular cases and about cultural influences generally, which are particularly difficult to gauge, may well be tentative: few answers are likely to be absolutely final.

Acknowledgements
Particular thanks are due to Patricia Howard, Colin Jones, Anne Laurence, Nick Levinson, Robert Philip, Kevin Wilson and Bruce Wood.

Introduction

This unit will discuss aspects of the impact of French culture in the British Isles, 1620–1714. Its overall aim is to consider the question: in what areas and to what extent did French culture penetrate life in the British Isles during this period? By culture, in this unit, is chiefly meant the culture of the court and the nobility: works and artefacts of high refinement, mainly architectural, literary and musical, commissioned or created under royal or noble patronage. This is sometimes known as 'high culture', as opposed to the 'culture' in a more general sense of the population at large. However, fashions in drama and clothing did reach a much wider public, sometimes filtered through the culture of the court and nobility, sometimes arriving more directly.

We enter here on a dimension of the course which is not even mentioned, much less discussed, by Coward or Briggs. Much of the unit is therefore given over to considering basic information. You will also be asked to engage actively with selected examples of primary evidence, printed and on video- and audio-cassette, in order to form your own impressions and draw your own conclusions. It is vital to base your arguments on the primary sources. These constitute the evidence which supports your conclusions.

The first point to be made is that although France did make a cultural impact on the British Isles in the seventeenth century, that impact was predominantly a one-way traffic (see *Anthology*, I.9), and remained so until the end of the period, when currents began to flow back from Britain to France in the early eighteenth century. This was the case across Europe generally, certainly in the second half of our period: monarchs and nobility from Lisbon to St Petersburg and from the Hague to Turin looked to Paris and Versailles for standards of artistic excellence. Throughout the century French statesmen were concerned with Britain as a neighbouring state and an important element in the international balance of power. But few Frenchmen or women, even diplomats, spoke English or were interested in British culture. Shakespeare was virtually unknown in France before the eighteenth century. French was the international language, having taken over from Latin.

The seventeenth century was not, of course, the first time that French cultural influences were felt in Britain. There had, to a greater or lesser degree, been a continuum of such influences of one kind or another since the Norman Conquest and during the Hundred Years' War.

Nor were such influences spread uniformly across the British Isles. Sixteenth-century Scotland with its direct contacts with France, was heavily influenced, Ireland perhaps least of all. Nor were such influences felt evenly down through society. Most people in Britain were probably quite unaffected by them.

In the sixteenth century and for most of the seventeenth, Britain was a recipient of foreign cultures rather than an exporter of her own. Before the Restoration of 1660, French was just one of several foreign influences which left their mark on British culture. While James VI and I and Charles I, following the example of contemporary monarchs abroad, made a point of patronizing the arts, French models were not the only or even the main ones. Artists, craftsmen and musicians from Italy and the Low Countries, as well as Frenchmen, were active at court. Under James I and Anne of Denmark, the Mortlake tapestry works were founded on the model of Henri IV's Gobelins factory at Paris: but the chief designer was a German, and the main court painters were Flemish and Dutch. The leading architect, Inigo Jones, who designed the Banqueting House at Whitehall (see TV1) and the Queen's House at Greenwich, and probably advised on the rebuilding of Wilton House for the Earl of Pembroke (see TV2) was influenced by the Italian, Palladio. Jigginstown, the great mansion near Dublin built by the Earl of Strafford as Lord Deputy in Ireland (see TV2), was modelled on Italian baroque styles. Charles I, a connoisseur of great refinement, built up the magnificent royal collection by purchasing paintings of the Italian and Flemish schools (see *Anthology*, I.8); and the main influence on English painters was that of two Flemish masters, Peter Paul Rubens, who painted the ceiling panels of the Banqueting Hall, and Anthony Van Dyck, who became principal court portraitist. Charles I did commission a statue of himself on horseback from the French sculptor, Hubert Le Sueur, Sculptor of the Royal Works since 1619 (the statue, in bronze, Britain's first equestrian statue, is at Charing Cross); but he also retained Italian sculptors.

Cromwell employed the Flemish portraitist, Peter Lely, whom Charles II retained to depict the ladies of his court, and who was followed as principal court artist by the German artist, Gottfried (later Godfrey) Kneller.

So the evidence does not suggest that the impact of French culture was predominant before the Restoration.

French culture in Restoration Britain

Exercise   The impact of French culture on the English court reached its height under Charles II. From your study of the course materials, can you suggest why?

Discussion   There are two related reasons. First, the long exile abroad of Charles and his court, particularly in France, and their exposure to French culture on the continent. Second, the unrivalled contemporary prestige across Europe of the court of Louis XIV, reflected in the artistic splendours of Versailles (which you will recall from TV1), the building and decorating of which coincided with Charles II's reign.

As a result, French was spoken at Charles's court and in high society. Leading writers and intellectuals, such as John Evelyn, Samuel Pepys and John Dryden, prided themselves on their knowledge of French. Mary Astell claimed that '... the French tongue is understood by most ladies' (*Anthology*, III.20, p.207). Sermons at court were often given in French. Charles's mother, Henrietta-Maria, was herself French (the daughter of Henri IV and Marie de Medici, and aunt of Louis XIV, who was thus Charles's cousin). Having spent part of his exile in France, Charles returned with an indiscriminate passion for things French, including a taste for French attire: large wigs and large hats with lace and feathers (see Fig. 31). He ordered his clothes from Paris. One of his mistresses, Mademoiselle de Kéroualle, whom he made duchess of Portsmouth, was French. He idolized the style and magnificence of Louis XIV, envied his absolute power, secretly admired his religion (which he probably adopted on his deathbed) and tried to emulate his cultural achievements as far as his far more limited means would allow. Like Louis, he patronized the stage. His musical tastes were modelled on those of Louis: he had a royal string orchestra of 24 violins, which played while he dined 'after the manner of France' (quoted in Spink, 1992, p.62) and which also performed orchestrally accompanied anthems in the chapel royal in imitation of the grand motets of Louis's court composer, Lully.

Christopher Wren and the impact of French architecture

Charles II also admired French architecture. He shared the view of his principal architect, Christopher Wren, who was in France during the construction of the new wing of the Louvre, and of Versailles, and who concluded that 'architecture has its political use, public buildings being the ornament of a country' (Clark, 1934, p.372). After the Great Fire of London in 1666, Charles had, in theory, an ideal opportunity to remodel the capital according to the ambitious designs which Wren drew up for this purpose, with long, broad, straight avenues, intersected by spacious squares, and adorned with large, stately public buildings. The realization of these plans, however, was beyond his means. Unlike Louis, Charles was never in a political position to override the rights of private landowners (which required parliamentary legislation), or financially capable of buying them out. As it was, parliament constantly queried his expenditure; and Charles was encumbered by his father's debts, his own debts and a national debt of £3,000,000 incurred under the Commonwealth. Hence public building in England could never match the scale or lavishness of Louis's achievements. It was more often the work of wealthy individual nobles, or of corporate bodies such as the Universities of Oxford and Cambridge and the Church of England.

Yet British taste in architecture, as in other arts, followed French. Sir Roger Pratt, one of the most influential English architects of the mid-century, advised anyone thinking of building to 'get some ingenious gentleman who has seen much of that kind abroad and been somewhat versed in the best authors of architecture ... to do it for you, and to give you a design of it in paper' (Thornton, 1978, p.5). Pratt's recommendation underlines the lack of native institutions for training in the arts and the consequent incentive to travel abroad. There were no British equivalents to the French *académies* until 1711, when Kneller founded an academy of painting in London. Whoever held himself out as a man of culture, therefore, was expected to have made the 'Grand Tour', including a visit to France.

Figure 23
Construction of north wing of
the Louvre, engraving.
Bibliothèque Nationale de
France.

Exercise   Read *Anthology*, III.31. What does Wren's letter indicate about his attitude
to French culture?

Discussion   Wren was clearly impressed by French architecture: specifically by the
north and east wings of the Louvre (see Fig. 23 and TV1), then in course
of construction. He visited the site daily, noting the scale and variety of
the works. He concluded that French architecture (including interior
decoration) was probably the best in Europe. He briefly met Bernini, saw
his design for the bust of Louis (Illustration Book, Pl.72), and was filled
with admiration for his plan for the Louvre (which was in the event
rejected in favour of that of Perrault), which he memorized.

(It is worth noting, as you can see from the fact that Wren met Bernini, an Italian, in Paris, that Italian influences increasingly reached
England from France rather than directly from Italy. French architects
like Lemercier built domes in Paris after seeing them in Rome. English
visitors to France were impressed by these architectural marvels and
imported them to England. So the English were not simply influenced by
French taste, but by French interpretations of Italian culture.)

Wren's sojourn in Paris (he also visited Versailles and Vaux-le-vicomte)
had a crucial and lasting effect on his own work as Surveyor of Works
from 1669 to 1718. There being no domes at all in England, what he saw
in Paris, notably Mansart's church of Val-de-Grâce, Lemercier's church of
the Sorbonne, and others, made a profound impression on him. On his
return to London in 1666, he submitted the first of successive proposals
to the commissioners for the rebuilding of St Paul's, destroyed in the
Great Fire: the new cathedral he suggested, should be surmounted by a
dome. In his report he referred admiringly to the domes he had seen in
Paris, 'constructed by the best artists', with whom he had had 'daily con-
ference' (Downes, 1988, p.9).

Wren's Sheldonian theatre at Oxford probably echoes the château of Vaux-le-vicomte (see TV2). Certainly his Royal Hospital at Chelsea was directly inspired by Les Invalides, with its famous domed chapel (the church of the Dome).

Figure 24
View and perspective of the Dome of Les Invalides, Paris, engraving after Joseph Aveline (c.1638–90). Photo: Roger-Viollet.

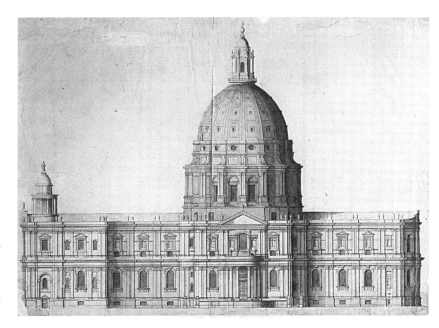

Figure 25
St Paul's, south front elevation. Study for complete design by Sir Christopher Wren. Codrington Library Wren Drawings II.29. Reproduced by permission of the Warden and Fellows of All Souls College, Oxford.

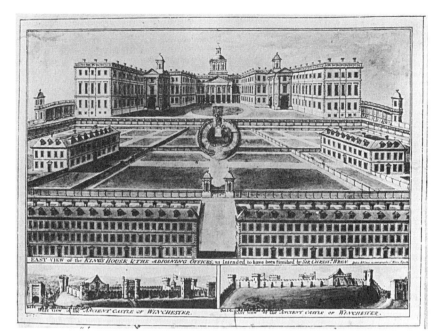

Figure 26
Engraving of Winchester Palace
'as intended to have been
finished', from John Milner,
The History, civil and
ecclesiastical, and Survey of
the Antiquities of
Winchester, *1798–1801.*
Building now demolished.
Photograph reproduced by
permission of Winchester City
Museums.

Exercise   Consider Figure 26, the palace which Wren built for Charles II at
Winchester (1683–5). (It was demolished in the nineteenth century.) Do
you detect any French influence?

Discussion   The palace (in the upper part of the picture) is recognizably influenced
by Versailles as remodelled by Le Vau (see TV1), which Wren also visited
in 1665. (Though considerably smaller than Versailles, Winchester has
been called 'the most French of all Wren's designs' (Harris, 1989, p.225),
and its scale was much bigger than that of most palaces and public buildings in Britain hitherto.) Wren learned from France that size and grandeur in themselves were potent symbols of monarchical prestige.
Enjoying at this time the support of a loyal Tory parliament, Charles was
able to indulge his taste for a palace obviously suggestive of the style of an
absolute monarch.

Wren, William III and Hampton Court

French influence can also be detected at Hampton Court, outside London, which (as you will recall from TV1) Wren rebuilt as a palace for William and Mary (*c.*1689–1700). Both in his original designs and in the
plans finally approved by William, Wren seemingly drew on his memories
of Paris and Versailles. He began with high hopes of being allowed to
raze all the old Tudor buildings to the ground and to build on the site
something entirely new – an English equivalent to Versailles.

Despite continual wars with France, William's own artistic tastes
were dominated by French models. He employed the nephew of André

Le Nôtre, Louis's landscape gardener at Versailles, to design his so-called Maestricht garden at Windsor. French workers at Hampton Court included Louis Laguerre, who painted the Labours of Hercules on the roundels in Fountain Court; Daniel Marot, the garden designer; and Jean Tijou, who produced the wrought-iron balustrade on the King's Staircase and an elaborate gateway in the park (all of which feature in TV1).

 Look at the park front of Hampton Court and the garden front at Versailles (shown in Video 12, Part 1). They are certainly similar in proportion though they differ in materials and most particularly in scale.

Wren was constrained in scope and materials, as Le Vau was not, by his master's economy. He was instructed to merge the new palace with the existing buildings. William was concerned with expenditure, and had no intention of clashing with parliament on money for Hampton Court; money for his wars with France was his overriding priority. (In addition, transport of Portland stone from the Isle of White was hindered by French mastery of the English Channel.) Besides, his tastes were Dutch as well as French, and it may be that what he genuinely wanted at Hampton Court was a compromise between French flamboyance and Dutch sobriety.

Ireland

The Royal Hospital, Kilmainham

The Royal Hospital at Kilmainham, Dublin (built for Charles II, 1680–6), like the subsequent Royal Hospitals at Chelsea and Greenwich, was avowedly modelled on Les Invalides, commissioned 10 years before by Louis XIV, from Libéral Bruant and Mansart, 1670–6. Charles's illegitimate son, the Duke of Monmouth, received drawings of Les Invalides from Louvois as early as 1671. The Duke of Ormond, Viceroy of Ireland, and others who had accompanied Charles during his exile in France, were impressed both by the function and the appearance of Les Invalides: as a home for war veterans and as an architectural monument to the glory of Louis XIV. According to an early account of Kilmainham, 'it is not to be doubted but from the excellency of that design [i.e. Les Invalides] first sprung the notion of building the like in this kingdom' (Thomas Wilson, 1713; quoted in McParland, 1985, p.1). Ormond made representations to Charles II around 1677, and Charles authorized the project by charter in 1679. The architect was Sir William Robinson, Surveyor-General since 1670.

Video Exercise You should now view Video 12, Part 2 and then answer the following questions.

1 In what specific ways does Kilmainham Hospital resemble Les Invalides?

2 Do you detect any markedly dissimilar feature?

Discussion   1(a) The purpose of the building. Neither Les Invalides nor the Royal
Hospital at Kilmainham was a hospital in the modern sense, though
each included an infirmary and dispensary. Both were designed as a
retirement home for several hundred needy, sick and disabled veterans, where, in the words of the Kilmainham charter, they might
'find a comfortable Retreat and a competent Maintenance'. The
founding of a permanent institution to house military veterans suggests the absolutist leanings of its founder. Such an institution
would serve the needs of the kind of standing army which both
Charles II and James II came close to instituting and which the
Commons so much dreaded. (And note that William and Mary also
commissioned a Royal Hospital at Greenwich (designed by Wren)
on the model of Les Invalides.)

(b) The scheme of an enclosed courtyard with arcaded covered walks.
These correspond to corridors on the floors above, and, like them,
provided ample space for walking, close to the Hospital, in all
weathers.

You may also have noted the semicircular upwards curve or 'crown'
over the chapel window, which resembles the same feature in the
centre of the main front of Les Invalides; the recessed carvings (in
pine at Kilmainham) above the entrance arches, with their dramatic
military motifs, crowded with details of trophies, as at Les Invalides;
the ornamental tribute to Charles in the form of two intertwined
letters 'C', in obvious imitation of Louis's analogous motif.

2(a) The scale of Les Invalides, Louis's biggest building project in Paris,
is far greater than at Kilmainham, reflecting the greater resources
available to Louis. Even so, Kilmainham was a large and ambitious
project by British standards.

(b) The chapel at Kilmainham contrasts with the chapel at Les Invalides
(i) in its location at the east wing of the building rather than in the
centre, as at Les Invalides. At Kilmainham, the dining hall, not the
chapel, forms the central architectural feature; (ii) in the relative
simplicity and sobriety of the chapel's exterior. In particular, the
chapel tower at Kilmainham (which was not added until 1701),
projecting through the roof of the pediment, contrasts markedly
with Mansart's enormous gilded dome at Les Invalides. A more simple, square tower erected at the end of William III's reign, was
thought appropriate for a Protestant chapel dedicated to the memory of Charles I.

(Paradoxically, the interior at Kilmainham chapel is more sumptuous and ornate than at Les Invalides. The carved woodwork at the
east end, in its richness and variety, and the elaborate plasterwork
on the compartmentalized ceiling, contrast with the dignified
sparseness of the chapel at Les Invalides.)

Charles financed the building of Kilmainham from a levy which he put
on the pay of the army of Ireland. The costs by 1686, when the Hospital

was virtually complete, totalled £23,500. While both institutions were intended to reflect glory on the founder monarchs, Kilmainham has nothing to compare with the huge recessed *bas-relief* equestrian monument to Louis XIV which dominates the centre of the front elevation at Les Invalides. (A *bas-relief* is a sculpture in which the figures project slightly from the background surface.)

The carving at Kilmainham was the work of a French Huguenot *émigré*, Jacques or James Tabary. After royal and aristocratic patronage of the arts, the arrival in Britain of expert craftsmen of every kind among the French Huguenot refugees in the late seventeenth century both before and after the revocation of the Edict of Nantes, must be reckoned one of the main factors in the spread of French models. By 1688 there were perhaps 80,000 French refugees in Britain, 30,000 of them in London alone (Réau, 1938, p.309). Tabary reached London in 1682 as an impoverished immigrant, receiving relief from the Threadneedle Street church. He settled in Ireland, where he seems to have prospered rapidly, being admitted as a freeman of Dublin the same year. Under Charles's Order in Council of 1679, the hospital building committee was authorized to 'send for artists, workmen and other persons, and after receiving proposals from them, to treat [i.e. negotiate] and agree'. The reason for the extraordinarily elaborate carving-work at Kilmainham Chapel may simply be that Tabary exceeded his commission. This was the conclusion reached by the governors of the Hospital. In 1687, when his work was complete, they recorded that he 'was not allowed the full value of his work in carving, framing and setting up the altar-piece, rail, panel and table in the chapel'. (Sir William Robinson, however, valued the altar-piece at £250, and payment to Tabary was authorized.) Here, then, is an example of the impact of French culture in the British Isles resulting partly from the enterprise and zeal of an individual French craftsman.

Ralph Montagu, Boughton, and the impact of French culture

Ralph Montagu (1638–1709), Earl and later first Duke of Montagu, is one of the most remarkable figures in the history of Anglo-French cultural relations in the seventeenth century. His main significance lies in his large-scale imitation and importation of French culture and taste and the development of a court style in England at the turn of the seventeenth and eighteenth century.

Like other royalists under the Commonwealth, Montagu lived abroad as a young man, returning to serve at Charles II's court after the Restoration. Charles appointed him as his ambassador to Louis XIV in 1666, and again from 1669–72, in 1676 and in 1677–8. Interestingly for such an enthusiast of French culture, Montagu was strongly anti-Catholic (which, however, did not inhibit him from accepting enormous gratuities from Louis which no doubt went to finance Montagu's francophile tastes). The family tradition was Puritan, but royalist. Because of his anti-Catholic views, Montagu supported the Exclusion Bill and the Duke of Monmouth and was implicated in the Rye House plot, after which he spent the years 1682–5 in exile in France. He remained out of favour under James II, during whose reign he began work on the transformation of his country seat at Boughton in Northamptonshire (*c.*1687–95). He

Figure 27
Ralph Montagu, later 1st Duke of Montagu (1638–1709), portrait by Benedetto Gennari, c.1678–9, oil on canvas, 87 cm x 70 cm oval. From the collection of the Duke of Buccleuch, KT, Boughton House, Northamptonshire.

returned to favour under William III, who conferred on him a viscountcy and an earldom.

Montagu's reception as the king's ambassador at Versailles was flattering from the first: Louis ordered that the fountains be played whenever Montagu was present. Versailles produced an immediate and lasting impression on him. According to Boyer, a seventeenth-century historian, 'Here it was that [he] formed his ideas in his own mind, both of buildings and gardening' (quoted in Cornforth, 1992, p.20). In 1674 Montagu purchased the Mortlake tapestry workshop, having in 1671 become Keeper of the King's Great Wardrobe (with responsibility for the decoration of the royal apartments). This gave him the opportunity to influence court taste directly, as well as to profit from his monopoly. Under William III, he was responsible for furnishing the royal palaces, including Hampton Court.

Montagu was a conspicuous purchaser of French luxury goods and a patron of French designs. He bought Boulle furniture and French carriages. He amassed a collection of French (and Italian) paintings. He built his town house, Montagu House, in Bloomsbury (on the site of the British Museum) and rebuilt it when it burned down, and his country house at Boughton – all three on the French model and with the help of French artists and craftsmen.

Figure 28
North prospect of Montagu House, engraving by James Simon, c.1714, 47 cm x 58 cm. Museum of London.

When the first Montagu House burned down in 1686, Montagu had it rebuilt by an architect brought over from France. The interior was decorated by French painters, carvers and gilders. Charles de la Fosse, who later gilded the dome of Les Invalides, painted ceilings both at Montagu House and at Boughton. For painting and furniture, wrote John Evelyn of Montagu House, 'there was nothing more glorious in England'

(Evelyn, 1955, p.497). (For an interior view of Montagu House, see Illustration Book, Pl.70.)

Montagu had a close circle of French friends, mainly Protestant refugees. They included the Frondeur poet and essayist, Charles de Saint-Evremond, and the physician, Pierre Sylvestre, who also became doctor to William III. Sylvestre must have been a man of unusual versatility. At Boughton, Montagu appointed him both as tutor to his son and as 'Inspector of Architecture and Gardens'. The playwright William Congreve dedicated *The Way of the World* (1700) to Montagu, stating that 'architecture and painting, to the great honour of our country, have flourished under your influence and protection' (Cornforth, 1992, p.22). Such outspoken praise suggests a tacit comparison of Montagu with the greatest patron of the age – Louis XIV (cf. *Anthology*, III.34) and perhaps a tacit contrast with the more parsimonious William III.

Boughton House

The Montagus had lived at Boughton since 1528; but the Tudor manor house was extended by Ralph Montagu in a wholly different style.

Exercise   Please look at Boughton on Video 12, Part 3. Do you notice any French influence in the style and layout of the house?

Discussion   Like Winchester Palace, which you considered earlier, Boughton gives the immediate impression of a palace in the French style, with its long open arcade on the ground floor, flanked by two pavilions. The north front above the arcade (or loggia) was built to provide a central suite of five state rooms for the reception of the sovereign (William III and his court visited Boughton in 1695) flanked by smaller suites in each pavilion for other important guests.

The architect is thought to have been Daniel Marot, who also designed the gardens at Hampton Court. The source for the design of the north front is believed to be by Jean Marot, the father of Daniel. Jean Marot's design, 'Profil d'une maison particulière de Paris' (profile of a private house in Paris) first published *c*.1654–60 was republished by Daniel Marot in *Nouveau livre des bâtiments* ('New book of buildings', Amsterdam, *c*.1700).

Exercise   Compare the north front of Boughton (Illustration Book, Pl.68 and Video 12, Part 3) with Pl. 71 in your Illustration Book, the design from Daniel Marot's book, and list any common features that you notice.

Discussion   1   The mansard roof.

2   The rustication on the arcade. (Rustication here means the heavily indented joints in the masonry.) The interior of the arcade at Boughton also contains such classic French features as busts of Roman emperors. These are supported on brackets and alternate with small round windows known as *oeil-de-boeuf* (bull's eye) windows.

3   The form of the windows in the two pavilions. These resemble typical French casements. (In fact the windows at Boughton are in the form of sash. Originally, each of the first floor windows contained 36 small panes, with heavy vertical bars in the centre. The nine windows of the state apartments were later fitted with more conventional English sashes, each containing 18 larger panes. The designer, however, was a Frenchman, Jean Pelletier.)

4   The columns between the windows on the first floor.

5   The dormer windows in the roof.

Figure 29
Elevation of the garden front of Versailles designed by Louis Le Vau, anonymous painting of the late seventeenth century showing the elevation before Mansart's addition of the Galerie des Glaces. Musée National du Château de Versailles. Photo: Réunion des Musées Nationaux Documentation Photographique.

Video Exercise   Now compare the north front of Boughton (Video 12, Part 3), with the garden front at Versailles (Fig. 29 and Video 12, Part 1). You will see that they too share at least two common features. What are they?

Discussion   1   The rustication on the arcade.

2   The columns between the windows.

Having considered Boughton generally and compared it with a design by Jean Marot and with a part of Versailles, we may reasonably conclude that Boughton draws on certain well-known elements in French architecture.

Exercise   We earlier considered evidence of the influence of Versailles at Hampton Court. It is possible that as well as designing the gardens at Hampton Court, Daniel Marot (as well as Christopher Wren) may also have influenced the exterior design of the palace. Let us now consider whether ideas employed at Boughton may in turn have influenced the interior design of Hampton Court. (We know, after all, that as Keeper of the King's Great Wardrobe, Montagu was responsible for furnishing Hampton Court.)

Compare the Great Staircase at Boughton (Video 12, Part 3) with the King's Staircase at Hampton Court (Video 12, Part 1), noting any similarities in design and decor.

Discussion   The two rooms are very similar in form.

1   On the ground floor there is the same rustication, on the first floor the same fluted Doric pilasters in *trompe l'oeil*. (*Trompe l'oeil*, literally 'deceives the eye', is a form of wall-painting which gives a three-dimensional effect when viewed from a distance.)

2   In both cases, the entrance leads up a grand staircase to a suite of royal apartments on the first floor.

3   In both cases there is a wrought-iron balustrade along the staircase. At Boughton the balustrade is based on a French design published in Henri Brisville's *Diverses pièces de serrureries* ('Different types of ironwork', 1663). At Hampton Court the craftsman was Jean Tijou.

4   In both cases, the walls are decorated with *trompe l'oeil bas-reliefs* of Roman military themes. Those at Boughton are by Louis Chéron, who had been a pupil of Charles Le Brun (who painted the ceilings at Versailles) at the Academy of Painting in Paris. His motifs at Boughton were inspired by the Arch of Constantine at Rome.

5   In both cases there are large-scale allegorical paintings of a type familiar at Versailles (see TV1), on the ceiling at Boughton, on the walls and ceiling at Hampton Court, portraying elaborate scenes from classical mythology. At Boughton, Discord throws the apple among the gods. At Hampton Court, in a rather complex allegory, based on Julian the Apostate's *Satire of the Caesars*, Alexander the Great, introduced to the banqueting gods by Hercules, symbolizes Protestant William, favoured by the gods above the Caesars, representing earlier Stuart kings.

The most dramatic of Chéron's ceilings at Boughton – in the Great Hall – is dominated by the figures of Hercules and Hebe, possibly symbolizing the marriage of William and Mary. Hercules is shown being rewarded for his labours by receiving the fruits of peace and love. Hercules may, however, be intended to represent Montagu himself (Murdoch, 1992, p.68). Whatever the correct interpretation, both at Boughton and at Hampton Court, classical imagery is clearly not merely decorative, but, as at Versailles, is intended to suggest contemporary analogies flattering to a patron.

Other common features include diamond-shaped tiles on the ground floor and a Roman-style bust above a door.

You may also have noted the same general interior design as at Hampton Court and Boughton in the picture of Montagu House (Illustration Book, Pl.70).

We thus see how French styles of interior design introduced by Ralph Montagu at Montagu House and Boughton may well have influenced the design of the royal palace at Hampton Court.

The grounds at Boughton

You may remember from TV2 that even the stable-block at Boughton suggests typical French influences (pavilions, triumphal arch, dome). Montagu appointed a Dutch gardener, Van der Meulen, to lay out the grounds (presumably under the supervision of Pierre Sylvestre).

Exercise   Now read *Anthology*, III.32, and remembering Montagu's first crucial impressions of Versailles, can you suggest a particular French influence in the grounds at Boughton?

Discussion   Visitors to Versailles were invariably impressed by the fountains (see also TV1 and Video 11). (The Latona fountain is shown in TV1.) We have noted that Louis XIV ordered them to be played whenever Montagu was there; and it is known that Montagu was anxious to install similar fountains at Boughton.

Montagu's first efforts were apparently unsuccessful. A contemporary writes of 'talk of vast gardens at Boughton; but I heard my Lord Montagu is very much concerned that the water, with which he hoped to make so fine fountains, hath failed his expectations' (Cornforth, 1992, p.22). By 1700 however, a succession of water gardens had been laid out, starting with a *Grand Etang* (Great Pool, still known as the 'Grandytang'). John Morton, describing Boughton in a book published in 1712 (*Anthology*, III.32), enthuses about the 'sumptuous water-works', the large pools or 'basins' and canals, the spectacular fountains or 'jets d'eaus' (the water spurting up to over 50 feet high) and cascades 'adorned with vases and statues'. (Unfortunately the fountains were later removed.)

Ralph Montagu was undoubtedly the most lavish and spectacular importer of French influences in Britain. His relative, the Duke of Somerset, designed Petworth house in Sussex on the model of the second Montagu House. Interest in French fashions in architecture and interior design was widespread among the nobility generally. Information about them entered the country in the form of pattern books containing illustrations and engravings. Daniel Marot published not only architectural illustrations, as we saw earlier, but also designs of the latest fashions in interior decoration, for example a book of prints published at Amsterdam (*c.*1695), entitled *Nouvelles cheminées à panneaux de glace à la manière de France* ('New glass-panelled chimney-pieces in the French manner'). The use of mirror-glass on walls and mantelpieces (the most splendid and lavish example of which in Europe, was, of course, the Hall of Mirrors at Versailles shown in TV1) became popular in aristocratic houses in Britain. Other innovations introduced from France included parquet flooring and interior shutters. Both are present at Boughton.

The impact of French language, literature and fashion

The theatre

Figure 30
Performance of Molière's Le Malade Imaginaire, *1674, engraving by Le Pautre, from I. Sylvestre,* Les Fêtes à Versailles, Troisième Journée, *1676. Bibliothèque Nationale de France. Photo: Bulloz.*

Suppressed under the Commonwealth, theatrical life recovered vigorously during the Restoration, with the cheerful support of Charles II and his courtiers, enthusiasts of the French theatre as patronized by Louis XIV. The conventions of the French theatre were introduced, such as elaborate scenery and the use of actresses instead of men or boys to play the female roles. In France, under Molière's influence, plays as well as operas were preceded by an overture (French *ouverture* = opening) and included incidental music, songs, choral music and short ballets. But such theatrical performances reached a much wider audience than king and courtiers. The theatre in Restoration England was patronized by people of many classes and was one of the means by which ideas about French culture, often mildly caricatured, reached a wider public.

Shakespeare and French theatrical taste

Exercise   Read *Anthology,* III.37 and consider Figure 30. What does *Anthology,* III.37 suggest about theatrical taste during the Restoration?

Discussion   You probably noted the following:

1   The musical element (which, by the way, is by Purcell) is very important. There is an orchestra of 24 violins (as in the king's own private orchestra). The play is preceded by an overture. (There are also Shakespeare's songs in the play, with harpsichord ('harpsicals') and theorbo accompaniment.)

2   Detailed attention is paid to elaborate and fanciful scenery (including a royal coat-of-arms, irrelevant to the play, and designed to draw attention to the patronage of the court), as well as functional scenery ('the scene') representing the tempest with which the play begins. There are also spectacular mechanical stage-effects, including ghosts, fire, thunder and lightning.

Although music and scenery had been an important accompaniment to plays (and especially to masques) under James I and Charles I, the large orchestra, elaborate scenery and special effects came in from France during the Restoration. The orchestra, no longer relegated to a minstrel's gallery, but placed between audience and stage, became an accepted constituent of theatrical performances into the reign of Queen Anne, and composers, notably Purcell, were commissioned to write incidental music for the theatre.

Shakespeare was unknown to seventeenth-century French audiences, the French theatre being dominated by Corneille, Racine and Molière. But even in England, Shakespeare's plays were adapted, indeed rewritten, being considered too crude and unpolished for post-Restoration audiences. After seeing a performance of *Hamlet,* John Evelyn noted that 'the old plays begin to disgust this refined age, since his Majesty's [Charles II] being so long abroad'. The text of *The Tempest* used in Shadwell's production was amended by William D'Avenant and by Dryden, and further 'improved' by Shadwell himself. Such adaptations tell us much about the influence of French critical taste.

    Listen to the arrangement for voice and harpsichord by Pelham Humphrey (who studied in France) of Ariel's song 'Where the bee sucks' from Shadwell's production of *The Tempest* (AC2, Section 6). Where Shakespeare wrote:

> On the bat's back I do fly
>
> Shadwell substitutes, as a more agreeable image:
>
> On a swallow's wings I fly

D'Avenant also adapted Shakespeare's 'dagger' speech from *Macbeth,* Act I, scene 1 (*Anthology,* III.33). You should read this now and, if you wish, compare it with the original. If you are familiar with *Macbeth,* you will see that in D'Avenant's version Shakespeare's language is shortened, simplified and altered in order to make the meaning more readily understandable and to suit contemporary theatrical taste. However, the effect seems to me to deprive the original of its strength.

Restoration critics found Shakespeare's language obscure (e.g. 'heat-oppressed brain', 'dudgeon' in the original *Macbeth*) and coarse and sought to change it. Dryden rewrote *Antony and Cleopatra* as *All For Love* (1678), replacing Shakespeare's blank verse with rhyming couplets throughout, in the manner of Corneille and Racine. They objected to a lack of 'poetic justice' in Shakespeare. Dryden complained that in *Troilus and Cressida* 'the chief persons ... are left alive; Cressida is false and not punished' (Nicoll, 1967, p.174). Nahum Tate, poet-laureate under William III, wrote a happy ending for *King Lear,* which replaced the original in theatrical performances into the nineteenth century.

Restoration critics also complained that Shakespeare did not conform to the rules of neo-classical tragedy observed in French drama. Lord Sheffield rewrote *Julius Caesar* in order to preserve the unity of time, in accordance with the rule requiring the action of the play to be complete within 24 hours. They found Shakespeare's plots, especially in his comedies, either too thin or too complicated and chaotic. They tidied up the plots and added new characters. In his version of *The Tempest,* discussed above, Shadwell introduced two extra characters, Hippolito and Dorinda, to balance Prospero and Miranda.

Many of these adaptations were performed well into the eighteenth century, indicating the tenacity with which French standards of 'correctness' and 'taste' took root in Britain.

Restoration comedy and French influences

Of all contemporary foreign playwrights known in Britain in the period of the Restoration, Molière, was the most popular and is traditionally thought to have had most impact on the English stage, both through translations of his comedies and in adaptations by Shadwell, Dryden and others (notably Dryden's *Amphitryon* (1690) from the original of the same name) and generally through the use which English dramatists made of his plots, ideas and techniques. An English version of Molière's *Tartuffe,* subtitled *The French Puritan* (1670) also owed its success to its appositeness in the contemporary climate of reaction to puritanical severity under the Commonwealth. Echoes of Molière have been traced in the plots of many Restoration comedies, for example William Wycherley's *The Country Wife* (1673) and *Plain Dealer;* Congreve's *Double Dealer* (1694) and *The Way of the World* (1700), Vanbrugh's *The Relapse* and Farquhar's *Beaux' Stratagem* (1707), though recent scholarship tends to regard Molière's influence as superficial.

Restoration drama can be of particular use to us here for the evidence it suggests of French influence in contemporary English life, to which the plays contain many references. Part of a scene in Vanbrugh's *The Provoked Wife* (1697) was actually written in French, suggesting, for one thing, that French was understood by the audience.

Wycherley's *The Gentleman Dancing-Master* (1671), though based on a Spanish original, includes the character of Mr Paris, an English fop newly returned from France and posing as a Frenchman, 'Monsieur de Paris'. According to Miles (1910, p.156), Paris is based on the character of Sganarelle, who appears in several of Molière's plays.

Exercise   Read *Anthology*, III.36 and consider it as evidence of French influence on English life.

Discussion   Since the character of Paris is avowedly satirical and exaggerated, it would be unsafe to rely on Wycherley's evidence alone. It may be assumed that few such persons as Monsieur de Paris existed in real life. On the other hand, as we know, there were many British travellers in France, as refugees under the Commonwealth (like Wycherley himself) and as tourists and scholars during the Restoration (like Wren), so that Wycherley's satire would have been lost on his audience had the French influences (fashions in clothes, food, music, language, snuffboxes) brought back by such visitors and referred to in the play not existed. (There are similar references in Etherege's *The Man of Mode* (1676).) We know of the impression which 'the new Louvre' made on Wren. Evidence of the import of French fashions is in fact corroborated by such memoirists as Pepys.

The model of Louis XIV and the French language

Exercise   Read *Anthology*, III.34. What does the extract suggest about the cultural impact of Louis XIV in Britain?

Discussion   The extract indicates the respect in which Louis was held among the cultural élite in Britain. Dryden was poet laureate under Charles II and James II, and became a convert to Catholicism, falling from favour for this reason after 1688. While acknowledging that Louis must be reckoned Britain's enemy during the war, he holds him up as a patron of the arts. Perhaps here (as with Congreve's dedication of *The Way of the World* to Montagu) there is an implied reflection on the less bountiful William III. The reference to Boileau, France's leading neo-classical poet and arbiter of literary taste in prose and verse, demonstrates Dryden's admiration for French standards of correctness; Dryden in turn dictated standards of literary taste in England.

Exercise   Read *Anthology*, III.35 (A) and (B). How reliable do you think these extracts are likely to be as evidence of the impact of the French language in Britain?

Discussion   Addison's anti-French views are plain from his outspoken remarks in *Anthology*, III. 35(A). As a Whig and a Protestant, he regards Louis XIV's military expansionism and economic protectionism as a menace to Britain. In *Anthology*, III.35(B), he complains of the influx of French military terms into the English language. We should be on our guard for exaggeration, given Addison's obvious hostility to France and the fact that *The Spectator* was the leading Whig satirical periodical in the reign of Queen Anne. We are not told whether the letter 'from the young gentleman in the army to his father' is genuine or fictitious. Like Wycherley's Mr Paris, however, even if the letter was invented to illustrate Addison's complaint of linguistic innovation, in order to have had any point as the butt of satire, it cannot have been too remote from actuality. In fact, it turns out to be remarkably accurate. Of the military terms cited by Addison, *chamade* and *cartel* first appear in English in 1684 and 1692 respectively; and *reconnoitre, maraud, corps, gasconade* and *charte blanche* between 1701 and 1711 during the war of the Spanish succession, just as Addison claims.

Note the naturalization of the French words *parterre* (1639) and *jet d'eau* (1706) in *Anthology*, III.32, written at much the same time as Addison's article. The survival in modern English of words as diverse as 'dessert' (1600), 'cravat' (1656), 'fatigue' (1669), 'engineer' (1702), 'refugee' (1685), whether newly imported or given a fresh lease of life in the seventeenth century, testifies to the lasting impact of French culture. English prose was also affected by French examples and the precepts of Boileau (mentioned in *Anthology*, III.34): it became simpler, more precise and lucid and flexible, better fitted for controversy and narrative, pre-eminently in the literary criticism of Dryden, of Addison himself in his 'essays' in *The Spectator* and in the writings on science and philosophy for which England was beginning to become known.

For despite his Whiggish political views, it would be quite wrong to imagine Addison, culturally speaking, as an ignorant John Bull. Far from it. Addison learned French in France, where he met several savants, including Boileau. He was steeped in the language and literature, which he greatly admired. His character-sketches in *The Spectator* have been attributed to the influence of La Bruyère (whose *Characters* were examined in Unit 13).

French musical influences

With Charles II's imitation of Louis XIV in the establishment of 24 violinists at court and in the Chapel Royal, the violin replaced the viol at court and the word 'fiddler' ceased to be a term of reproach, associated with taverns. Charles, who liked the gaiety and rapidity of French music and the court ballets of Lully, composer to Louis XIV, sent one musician, Pelham Humphrey, to France to study under Lully; according to Pepys, he returned to England 'an absolute Monsieur' (Anthony, 1973, p.106). Earlier we noted Humphrey's setting of a Shakespeare song. A French pupil of Lully, Louis Grabu, was put in charge of Charles's violinists and became Master of the King's Music in 1665.

Opera

Opera was, in Dryden's definition, 'a poetical tale, or fiction, represented by vocal and instrumental music, adorned with scenes, machines and

dancing' (Dent, 1928, p.161). It came to England both directly and
indirectly from France. *Ariane, ou le Mariage de Baccus* (1659), an opera by
Robert Cambert (libretto by Pierre Perrin), was performed in London in
1673 to celebrate the marriage of the Duke of York to Mary of Modena. A
French company performed Lully's *Cadmus et Hermione* (words by
Philippe Quinault) in London in 1686. The music was considered 'indeed very fine' (Anthony, 1973, p.106). A handful of English operas followed, modelled on the creations of Lully, Quinault and Molière. At the
same time, opera in Britain also developed from the hybrid genre of
music and drama established by Shadwell's production of *The Tempest*
(1674), with its substantial musical elements. Opera also received a boost
from royal patronage. Charles II, having failed to secure a visit to London
by the French court opera company, commissioned Louis Grabu to com-
pose an opera and Dryden to write the libretto. This was *Albion and
Albanius*, completed in 1685 and celebrating Charles as 'the best of
kings', just as Lully and Molière glorified Louis XIV in similar terms.
Albion and Albanius, the first full-length all-sung opera in English, is a
tragédie lyrique 'in the French manner through and through' (Caldwell,
1991, p.576), following the model of Lully, with an overture played by a
string orchestra scored in five parts. Until the eighteenth century, however, opera was confined to performance at court and in private houses.

Henry Purcell is generally regarded as the first native English musical genius, emancipated from foreign influence. The following excerpt
from the dedication of the opera *Dioclesian* (1690), which Purcell wrote to
Dryden's libretto shows that Purcell feels that British music, though
promising, is still in its 'nonage', retains its 'barbarity' and has much to
learn from French and more especially Italian examples. (The dedication
was probably 'ghosted' by Dryden.)

> Musick is yet but in its Nonage, a forward Child, which gives hope
> of what it may be hereafter in *England*, when the Masteres of it shall
> find more encouragement. 'Tis now learning *Italian*, which is its
> best Master, and studying a little of the *French* Air, to give it some-
> what more of Gayety and Fashion. Thus being farther from the Sun,
> we are of later Growth than our Neighbour Countries, and must be
> content to shake off our Barbarity by degrees. The present Age
> seems already dispos'd to be refin'd, and to distinguish betwixt wild
> Fancy, and a just, numerous Composition. (from dedication of
> *Dioclesian* to Charles Seymour, Duke of Somerset (relative of that
> other patron of the arts, Ralph Montagu); in Price, 1984, p.204)

You will recall that we noted earlier the popularity in Britain of the
French overture. If we compare Lully's overture to *Thésée* (1685) with
Purcell's overture to *Abdelazar, or the Moor's Revenge* (1695) (AC2, section
6), the following striking similarities emerge:

1   In each case the overture begins with a slow section, followed by a
     fast section.

2   In each case the opening section is characterized by dotted
     rhythms. The slow section begins in the manner of a fugue (a com-
     position based on a repeated theme, with a contrapuntal texture).

3   The instruments are predominantly strings.

Figure 31
The Future Charles II
dancing with his sister at a
ball in The Hague, *painting
by Cornelius Jannsens. The
Royal Collection © Her Majesty
Queen Elizabeth II.*

Purcell's best-known opera, *Dido and Aeneas* (*c.*1683/4), also begins with
an overture in the French style. The balletic duet and chorus, 'Fear no
danger to ensue' in *Dido and Aeneas* is recognized as the item most
influenced by French example (Price, 1984, p.249). On the other hand,
Dido's well-known lament, 'When I am laid in earth' is described as cast
'in the utterly conventional Italian operatic lament' (Price, 1984, p.258).

The arrival in Britain of Handel and Bononcini under Queen Anne
marks the displacement of French by Italian opera as the crucial influence on the progress of opera in Britain.

Charles II brought formal French dancing into fashion in Britain.
Innumerable court balls were held in his reign. The dances were mostly
in the classic French styles which continued throughout the eighteenth
century: the *branle, courante* and minuet (in which the Duke of Monmouth was said to shine).

Conclusion

French cultural influences in Britain, though also felt before and after,
were at their height under the later Stuarts (*c.*1660–1714). But there were
also influences from other cultures, notably Italian and Dutch. Nor were
French influences felt evenly across Britain or down through society. The
vast majority of people were probably not affected by it at all. French culture reflected the taste of individual monarchs, of wealthy and aristocratic
patrons, such as Ralph Montagu, and of the cultural élite in general,
though caricatures of French people and fashions were widely publicized
through the theatre and the popular press.

There were important limits to the monarchs' powers of patronage. No British ruler could build upon Louis's grand scale. Charles II could not enact Wren's plans to rebuild London or even Whitehall. He depended for funds on parliament's consent. Neither was William III in a position to sanction Wren's original plans for Hampton Court, even assuming that he aspired to anything as grandiose. British monarchs also needed the co-operation of the office of Office of Works to commission public buildings, like St Paul's. Neither parliament nor the bureaucracy was co-operative. The aristocratic grandees, Whig and Tory, were better placed than constitutional monarchs to initiate ambitious building schemes and emulate continental tastes on their own estates. Wren's modest Kensington palace, built for William III, was outshadowed not only by Blenheim palace, which Vanburgh built for the Duke of Marlborough, authorized by act of a grateful Whig parliament after his great victory over the French in 1704, but also by Castle Howard, which Vanburgh built for the Earl of Carlisle. Chatsworth in Derbyshire, designed by William Talmon for the Duke of Devonshire, has been described as 'the first great Whig palace' (Hook, 1976, p.141).

Exercise   Relying on your reading in this unit and its associated material, consider the following question. In what areas of life and by what means do you think French culture made its deepest impact?

Discussion   French influences affected architecture, decoration, painting, literature, social fashion, language and music. It came in two interrelated forms: the wholesale importation of commodities from France, including the commissioning of French artists and craftsmen; and the imitation of French models. It would be difficult to exaggerate the importance of the influence in Britain of French Huguenot refugee artists and craftsmen, such as Marot, Tabary, Tijou, Laguerre and Chéron. It is ironical that by his policy on religious uniformity Louis XIV should unintentionally have benefited his enemies (as Saint-Simon noted, *Anthology*, III.8). As for the depth of impact, some French influences were ephemeral. English opera on the French model was particularly short-lived, and was soon overtaken by Italian models.

The popularity of French high culture coexisted with bad political and economic relations between Britain and France.

From the excerpts from Dryden and Addison (*Anthology*, III.34 and 35), it is clear that while Louis XIV was associated with religious persecution, absolute power and megalomaniac ambitions to dominate Europe, 'he was also the centre of the most magnificent court in Europe which was still the undisputed leader of fashion and culture' (Ede, 1979, p.42). French culture continued to be accepted in Britain as the supreme standard of taste, nor did war mean the severance of diplomatic relations, despite long periods of hostilities between France and Britain (1689–97 and 1701–13). Even during Louis's Dutch War (1672–9), William, as Prince of Orange, had ordered his clothes from Paris; and as king of England, at the height of the War of the Spanish Succession, he ordered, through his ambassador at Versailles, the latest French beds (Clark, 1934, p.373; Jackson-Stops, 1992, p.57). As Coward (p.342) says, 'William's admiration for French culture was as great as his determination to halt and reverse these French gains' (i.e. Louis's conquests).

On the other hand, there was a simultaneous undertow, a national reaction against French models particularly after the revolution of 1688 and with Britain's spectacular victories over France during the War of the Spanish Succession. The Earl of Shaftesbury, Whig politician and writer on aesthetics, and Colen Campbell in his influential collection of architectural plates, *Vitruvius Britannicus,* the first volume of which appeared in 1715, held up Palladio and Inigo Jones (allegedly reflecting the values of republican Rome), rather than Le Vau and Mansart, as the proper models for British architects; and Whig grandees in the early eighteenth century tended to reject French styles when designing their houses, as much for ideological as for aesthetic reasons. (Compare the note of national as well as cultural triumphalism in Addison, *Anthology,* III.35.)

For this reason, the Whigs constantly hampered Wren's work on St Paul's; while the Tories, on returning to power in 1710, commissioned 50 new churches for London, blocked funds earmarked for the building of Blenheim palace and dismissed Vanburgh as Controller of Works.

Throughout the period, and even when the impact of French culture was at its height, there were influences other than French, notably Dutch and Italian. Take architecture and interior design. While Ralph Montagu intended Boughton to mirror Versailles, his cousin, John Cecil, Lord Exeter, designed Burghley House, near Stamford, in the Italian manner; and Burley-on-the-hill in Rutland, seat of Daniel Finch, second earl of Nottingham, reflects both French and Italian influences (see TV2). Hugh May (1622–84), one of the leading influences on English post-Restoration domestic architecture, spent the Interregnum in Holland, befriended the Dutch artist, Lely, and on his return found commissions for the great Dutch carver, Grinling Gibbons. Brick, as well as stone, was used at Hampton Court, after the Dutch model. The sash-window, effective for excluding drafts, was introduced from Holland, and made an early appearance at Hampton Court. Dutch tiles became especially popular. At Hampton Court, Queen Mary had a complete room faced with tiles. She also introduced from her palace at Het Loo in Holland the use of china ware as a form of interior decoration popular to this day. Beaulieu House in Ireland (see Video 5) was wholly Dutch in inspiration.

Yet even those who were not primarily exponents of French culture, sooner or later tended to come under its influence. Sir William Bruce visited Holland in 1658, but the style he adopted in his extension of Holyrood House for Charles II (TV1), reflected the models which he had seen during a visit to France in 1663. Van der Meulen, Montagu's Dutch gardener at Boughton, constructed a system of fountains on the model of Versailles. And by the end of the century, the most prominent carvers, such as Tabary, were French. Even Italian styles tended to reach Britain via France. The Italian painter, Verrio, who came to Britain in 1674 with Ralph Montagu to work at Burghley House, had trained for several years in France.

And many Dutch craftsmen themselves worked in France or were influenced by French styles. Daniel Marot, the *émigré* French architect, worked for William III in Holland, before designing the gardens at

Hampton Court. Het Loo itself, with its formal 'Dutch' garden and fountains, is partly modelled on Versailles.

Exercise   From your study of the course materials, can you outline any important French influences which did not take root in Britain?

Discussion   You may have noted the following.

1   Religion. Even those most influenced by French culture, such as Ralph Montagu and Joseph Addison (*Anthology*, III.35 (A)), were hostile to the Roman Catholic faith. Charles II and James II were the exceptions. The 1688 Revolution saw a vehement reaction against Roman Catholicism, which was associated with superstition, tyranny and the persecution of Protestants. William and Mary and Queen Anne were seen as protectors of Protestantism at home and abroad (remember the carved pediment above the garden front at Hampton Court).

2   Absolutism. Again, while Charles II and James II had absolutist leanings, both were dependent on parliament. The Whig supporters of William III acclaimed the Glorious Revolution as the triumph of constitutional government against oppressive absolutist rule (Addison, *Anthology*, III.35 (A) again). Louis's absolutism was associated with a standing army and the ambition to tyrannize over Europe, while British rule was associated with the defence of 'liberty' at home and abroad. (Again this is symbolized in the pediment at Hampton Court.) The contrast is expressed in a birthday ode for William by the poet laureate Nahum Tate, to celebrate the Peace of Ryswick in 1697:

> Such was Europe's late Distress,
> When for the suffering World's Repose,
> With equal Courage and Success,
> Our Second Hercules arose.

3   Science and philosophy. French scientific and philosophical thought in the seventeenth century, based on deductive rationalism from general abstract principles and associated with Descartes, made little impact in Britain (though Hobbes had contact with Descartes and other French thinkers in the early seventeenth century – and their names were familiar to Mary Astell – see *Anthology*, III.20 (C) and AC2, section 5). In the second half of the century it was inductive empiricism and experimentation in Britain that produced the most impressive results in the discoveries of Newton and his contemporaries in the Royal Society (founded 1660) and established British scientists and philosophers (e.g. Locke) as leaders in the field.

It could thus be plausibly argued that French influence in Britain was essentially superficial and related to externals, to the arts, architecture and social fashion, without affecting the underlying structure of church, state and society. On the other hand, we also need to bear in mind that we are dealing with the culture of the ruling minority who determined Britain's affairs, the propertied classes of those with an income of over £100 a year: the peers, bishops, baronets, knights, esquires, gentlemen, office-holders, merchants, lawyers. These, it was calculated by one Gregory King in the 1690s, amounted to just over 3 per cent of the population. For this reason, it can be argued that it is important to study their cultural background.

As stated at the beginning, the import of French culture into seventeenth-century Britain was largely a one-way traffic. Britons travelled to France in order to learn what was considered the best and most fashionable; foreign travel was a form of education. English was not spoken abroad. French scientists could not read the *Transactions* of the Royal Society. Montagu's friend, the French writer Saint-Evremond, who lived in England as a political refugee for over forty years from 1662 to 1703 and is buried in poets' corner at Westminster Abbey, did not trouble to learn English. Towards the end of Louis XIV's reign, however, there began the cross-fertilization of French thought by British, which was to become a marked feature of the eighteenth-century French Enlightenment. A reaction set in among some French thinkers to absolutism and the power of the Catholic church. (In Unit 13 we noted a critical attitude towards aspects of Louis's rule among some French commentators.) Huguenot *émigrés* not only employed their skills as craftsmen in the British Isles, but also transmitted back to France, in translation, information about British life and culture. One such refugee, Pierre Coste, translated Locke, Newton and Shaftesbury, introducing them for the first time to a French readership. There gradually developed a growing admiration for the British amalgam of constitutional government, religious toleration, freedom of the press and for the economic prosperity and cultural and scientific efflorescence in the reign of Queen Anne which they were thought to promote. The manifesto of the impact on France of British culture was Voltaire's *Letters on the English* (1733), which has in turn been described by Gustave Lanson as 'the first bombshell thrown against the *ancien régime*' in France.

References

Anthony, J.R. (1973), *French Baroque Music from Beaujoyeulx to Rameau*, Batsford, London.

Caldwell, J. (1991), *The Oxford History of English Music,* vol.I, Oxford University Press, Oxford.

Clark, G.N. (1934), *The Later Stuarts*, Oxford University Press, Oxford.

Cornforth, J. (1992), 'Boughton: Impressions and People' in T. Murdoch (ed.), *Boughton House. The English Versailles,* Faber and Faber, London.

Dent, E.J. (1928), *Foundations of English Opera. A Study of Musical Drama in England during the Seventeenth Century,* Cambridge University Press, Cambridge.

Downes, K. (1988), *The Architecture of Wren*, Redhedge, Reading.

Ede, M. (1979), *Art and Society in England under William and Mary,* Staines and Bell, London.

Evelyn, J. (1955), *The Diary of John Evelyn,* edited by E. S. de Beer, vol.IV, Oxford University Press, London.

Harris, J. (1989), 'The Architecture of the Williamite Court', in R.P. Maccubbin and M. Hamilton-Phillips (eds), *The Age of William III and Mary II. Power, Politics and Patronage 1688–1702,* The College of William and Mary, Virginia.

Hook, J. (1976), *The Baroque Age in England*, Thames and Hudson, London.

Jackson-Stops, G. (1992), 'French and Dutch Influence on Architecture and Interiors', in T. Murdoch (ed.), *Boughton House. The English Versailles*, Faber and Faber, London.

McParland, E. (1985), 'The Royal Hospital Kilmainham', *Country Life*, 9 and l6 May (Reprinted for the Irish Architectural Archive.)

Miles, D.H. (1910), *The Influence of Molière on Restoration Comedy,* Columbia University Press, New York.

Murdoch, T. (ed.) (1992), *Boughton House. The English Versailles*, Faber and Faber, London.

Nicoll, A. (1967), *A History of English Drama, vol.I. Restoration Drama 1660– 1700,* Cambridge University Press, Cambridge.

Price, C.A. (1984), *Henry Purcell and the London Stage,* Cambridge University Press, Cambridge.

Réau, L. (1938), *L'Europe française au siècle des Lumières*, Albin Michel, Paris.

Spink, I. (ed.) (1992), *The Seventeenth Century,* Blackwell History of Music in Britain, Blackwell, Oxford.

Thornton, P. (1978), *Seventeenth-Century Interior Decoration in England, France and Holland*, Yale University Press, New Haven.

Unit 15
Armies, materiel and finance

Prepared for the course team by Clive Emsley

Contents

Study timetable

Weeks of study	Texts	Video	AC	Set books
2	*Anthology*, III.38–44; Date Chart	Video 13		Coward, Briggs

You are advised to view again TV 5 and TV 6 during these two weeks.

Objectives

By the end of the unit you should have a knowledge and understanding of:

1   the wars involving France and the British Isles between 1660 and 1714;

2   developments in the organization and professionalization of the military during these years;

3   the practices developed to recruit soldiers and sailors, and above all, to finance war.

Introduction

You will be well aware, from your reading of the set books and from Units 11 and 12, that France and the British Isles were involved in major wars against each other in the last third of the seventeenth and at the beginning of the eighteenth century. In Unit 12, Bill Purdue notes that making war and expanding France's frontiers were the overriding aims of Louis XIV, and he equates Britain's arrival as a great power with her development of a navy to rival that of France, and an army capable of intervening on the continent. Of course, it was the princes, and their governments, who made the decisions about involvement in international wars; but the burdens of the wars in the form of taxation and the demand for men to fight them, fell on their peoples.

The nature and incidence of war, 1660–1714

As a major continental land power France had been heavily involved in the European wars of the first half of the seventeenth century. In contrast, even though she experienced her own civil wars and British soldiers (by which I mean English, Irish, Scots and Welsh) had fought in a variety of continental armies, Britain had largely kept out of European conflicts. Between 1660 and 1714 the French involvement remained much as it had been as Louis XIV strove to advance his frontiers and increase his dependants, but the British experience – and remember that the 'power' at war was England – changed. For England/Britain there were wars against the Dutch in 1664–6 and 1672–4, while from 1689 to 1714, with only a brief respite (1697–1702), she was engaged in the coalitions against Louis XIV. This conflict against France marked the beginning of a series of struggles between the two which were to be fought across the globe, and which continued until the decisive wars of the French Revolution and Napoleon (1793–1815).

The wars in the second half of the seventeenth century were fought by armies which were increasing in numbers, and increasingly more professional in their recruitment and training. Infantry grew in numbers at the expense of cavalry. The pike virtually disappeared from the battlefield; infantrymen armed with muskets transformed these into thrusting weapons for close quarters fighting by using a new invention, the bayonet. Musketry and artillery made battles extremely costly in human lives, ten to twenty-five per cent casualties were not unknown; consequently, during the campaigning season of the spring and summer, generals sought to outmanoeuvre their opponents bringing them to battle only on the most favourable terms. Strategists sought to construct impregnable fortresses in key positions to defend their own territory, from which invasions could be launched, and from which their own armies could be supplied and troops sent out to harass an enemy. Improved fire-power and fortifications resulted in a preponderance of sieges over battles and generals sought to outmanoeuvre their opponents rather than always bring them to battle. In the 1670s one experienced British soldier, Roger Boyle, earl of Orrery, noted:

> Battells do not now decide national quarrels, and expose countries to the pillage of the conquerors, as formerly. For we make war more like foxes, than lyons; you will have twenty sieges for one battell. (quoted in Parker, 1988, p.16)

John Churchill, duke of Marlborough, fought only four major battles in his ten campaigns (Blenheim, 1704; Ramilles, 1706; Oudenarde, 1708; Malplaquet, 1709) but he also conducted thirty sieges.

Figure 32
Battle of Blenheim, one of the duke of Marlborough's major battles, 1704. (Mansell Collection)

Exercise   Turn now to *Anthology*, III.38, read it (and you will probably find it useful to read it with reference to the map at the front of this block), and answer the following questions. (Illustration Book, Pl.74 shows the French border fortresses.)

1   What is Vauban recommending here?

2   In what way do Vauban's comments amplify the points discussed in the preceding paragraph?

3   What does Vauban propose for other older fortresses, and what advantages does he see from pursuing this policy?

Discussion   1   Vauban proposes two lines of fortresses along the new north-eastern frontier of France.

2   Vauban emphasizes that these fortresses can be used not only to defend France, but also to launch invasions into other territories.

3   He believes that the fortresses inside France are largely redundant and can, in time be destroyed; two advantages should accrue from this – first there will no longer be any internal strong points to be seized by rebels within the kingdom (indeed Vauban believes that such fortresses positively encourage potential rebels), and second, the removal of ten old fortresses will release 30,000 men from guard duty and for the battlefield.

Figure 33
Portrait of Sébastien Le Prestre de Vauban (1633–1707).
(Mansell collection)

Sébastien Le Prestre de Vauban (1633–1707) developed a formidable reputation as a military engineer and as the leading expert on the kind of siege warfare conducted by the armies of the late seventeenth and eighteenth centuries. As he promised in the concluding paragraph of his memorandum, he travelled to other frontier areas of France and recommendations from these areas also led to fortress building. Vauban was particularly keen to see the French frontiers straightened as far as possible to remove exposed salient and vulnerable enclaves. His proposals resulted in the permitted decay, or deliberate destruction, of some 600 fortresses and city walls within France, while 133 strongholds were built or rebuilt on, or close to, the frontiers. His fortresses proved their worth throughout the eighteenth century and beyond.

At this point I would like you to look at Video 13 where there is a discussion of how to 'read' seventeenth-century fortifications of the type built by Vauban.

Of course fortresses were sometimes captured by assault, or else forced to surrender after a long siege (note that Vauban was expecting to capture several key enemy fortresses in the next war); and some generals won victories on the battlefield while others lost, but decisive victory in war in Europe seemed to recede before what appeared to be an increasing stalemate. This stalemate, in turn, encouraged developments in war on the sea as a means of making a breakthrough; the increasing confrontations between the European powers in their embryonic colonial empires also contributed to a build up in battleships and navies. By the late seventeenth century the heavily armed battleship had become the most sophisticated weapon of war of the period, requiring tremendous skills on the part of both officers and men to sail them, navigate them, and fight them.

Armies and navies

Unit 14 assessed the impact of French culture on the British Isles. It described among other things, the way in which the military hospitals at Kilmainham and Chelsea were inspired by Les Invalides. The French led the way in Europe in many of the developments in armies during the seventeenth century. The process by which independent companies and regiments were brought under a centralized control was accelerated, but by no means completed, under Louis XIV. However, well before the end of the century, the regiments in his army were all uniformed, commonly accommodated in barracks (rather than in inns and private houses) when not on campaign, and subject to annual inspections. The army's pay and supply, while chaotic by modern standards, was put onto a more regular footing; the officers were organized in a clearly defined hierarchy, and while men could still purchase commissions, they had to pass qualifying tests. Recruitment and supply remained largely in private hands, but Richelieu had established the foundations for the civil administration of the royal army by deploying military *intendants* to supervise field armies in time of war and, subordinate to them, *commissaires* to supervise pay, equipment and supply. These foundations were built on by Louis XIV's two great ministers of war Michel Le Tellier (1603–85) who served from 1642 to 1668, and his son the Marquis de Louvois (1641–91), who succeeded his father serving from 1668 until his death. The ministry grew in size and authority under these men requiring regular reports from *intendants*, *commissaires* and even commanding officers; and while both men were tainted by the venality and nepotism typical of their times, they appointed able subordinates, notably, as military inspector, Jean Martinet, whose name subsequently became a synonym for a military disciplinarian, and, as principal military engineer, Vauban.

British military reforms followed in the wake of the French. There was no national army under the Restoration monarchy; however the separate English, Irish, and Scottish armies all served the same king, and personnel and formations could be exchanged. In emergencies the king could also call on the Anglo-Dutch Brigade, a group of English and Scottish regiments in the pay of the Dutch. During the decade of Anglo-Dutch wars the brigade was disbanded; it was re-established, however, in 1674. There was no training for officers; many men who took the career seriously travelled abroad and fought in foreign armies to learn the skills of their trade. Such officers were much prized by James II when he began to augment his army following Monmouth's Rebellion; and William III, understandably, put faith in the British officers whom he had known in the Anglo-Dutch brigade.

Louis XIV did not have to contend with a powerful legislative body which objected to the idea of a standing army; English monarchs did. Charles II had enlarged his army on three occasions: during the two wars against the Dutch, and for the projected war against France in 1678. On each occasion there were anxieties expressed in parliament, stimulated and amplified by the French example, that this army could be used to subvert the constitution and establish an arbitrary, absolutist government; there were further concerns that Charles was employing Catholic officers in the expanded army. However on each occasion, after the war or emergency, Charles disbanded his new soldiers and the anxieties subsided correspondingly. On the succession of James II, the English army consisted of just under 9000 men, the Irish army of 7500, and the Scottish army of just over 2000. The large grants which parliament gave to James in the summer of 1685 enabled him to enlarge his army, and the events of that year, notably Monmouth's Rebellion, convinced him of the need for a standing army. By the end of 1685 James had some 19,000 troops in England, including part of the Anglo-Dutch brigade, and not all of these were disbanded. James's proposals for his army brought him into conflict with his parliament.

Exercise   Turn now to *Anthology*, III. 39 and 40, read them, and answer the following questions.

1   What is the difference between the two kinds of document you are looking at here?

2   What was the political context of James's speech? (Reference back to Unit 11, or to Coward, pp.336–9, should jog your memory if you are stuck here.)

3   What is James seeking from parliament?

4   What are the key arguments deployed by James in his speech?

5   What impression does Sir John Bramston's account give you of the attitude in parliament towards James and his proposals?

6   What kind of information can you glean from Bramston's account which is not to be found in the *Parliamentary Debates*?

7   Do you think Bramston's accounts of the debates are reliable? and if so, why?

Discussion   1   One is a detailed report of the debates in parliament, the other is an extract from a personal memoir. (The former document is rather similar to, and in some respects is a forerunner of, the contemporary Hansard, but note that it was not published contemporaneously. The right to publish detailed reports of parliamentary proceedings was not secured until the late eighteenth century.)

2   James was addressing parliament in the aftermath of the rebellions of Argyll and Monmouth.

3   James wanted an augmented, regular army in place of the militia; he also wanted to be able to keep Catholic officers in the army in spite of the Test Acts.

4   James considered the militia as inadequate and ineffective, particularly in comparison with well-disciplined, regularly paid troops; he argued that he knew the Catholic officers, that they were loyal, that it would be a disgrace for them should they be dismissed, and that, finally, he was not prepared to be without them in the event of another rebellion.

5   Bramston's account suggests a lively debate first over James's request for a larger standing army and the effectiveness of a militia, and then over the Catholic officers. His description suggests, I think, some uncertainty on the part of the MPs – many were silent, Sir Richard Temple appears to have argued one way and voted another; but he also stresses the loyalty of the members to the king and what appears to have been a reluctance to criticize him – note the silence at the beginning of Saturday's debate, the 'tenderness and deference' shown towards James, and the decision not to use 'harsh' words about the Catholic officers.

6   Bramston's account gives an impression of the atmosphere in parliament and the feelings of the members which the detailed reports of speeches does not give. His comment on the silence at the opening of the debate is a good example of this.

7   These passages come from that section of Bramston's memoirs
        which was kept as a diary; it is therefore, probably, a reasonably
        reliable account of the proceedings. (Of course it would be wrong
        to rely on this as the sole source for what went on; but, in fact, other
        accounts tie in closely with Bramston's.)

I shall return to the question of the militia below ('Auxiliary forces'), and
shall concentrate for the moment on the Catholic officers. There is an
important question here which has exercised the minds of historians
since 1688 – what exactly was James trying to do in creating a standing
army and employing Catholic officers? Was he seeking to take England
down the road of continental absolutism, using his army as a coercive
force? James's English army remained overwhelmingly Protestant and it is
most unlikely that he could have created a Catholic army in England.
The earl of Tyrconnel, however, whom James put in command of the
Irish army did purge the Protestants in that force between 1685 and 1688.
The problem was that Tyrconnel finished up with a largely inexperienced
army. The new kind of war meant that discipline and experience were
important to enable men quite literally to stand up to volleys of musketry
and to manoeuvre on the battlefield. The general inexperience of Tyrconnel's men is one reason, perhaps, why the Jacobite army in Ireland
was defeated. As a professional soldier himself, James was aware of the
value of experience, and while he may not have set out to create a
Catholic army, he does seem to have been intent on creating a professional army which was loyal, first and foremost, to him. Of course, professionalism and centralization were the directions in which most
European monarchs and most European armies were moving at the time.
After weighing up the evidence the most recent historian of James and
his army concluded:

> The curious and unique circumstances of 1688 give the historian no
> reason for believing that James did not and could not have used his
> army to pursue his own personal policies. The army of James II was
> very different from that of his brother and was well advanced along
> the road to being an absolutist force by the time of William's inter-
> vention. Moreover, there is no substantial evidence that the army
> officers objected to being exploited in this way; the military
> rebellion of 1688 was not about the use of the army or the rights of
> the monarchy but about property. Nor was it too small to coerce the
> country. During the 1680s Louis XIV possessed a standing army of
> between 80,000 and 100,000 men to control a population of some
> twenty million; James II had an army of 20,000 to dominate a popu-
> lation that was no larger than five and a half million people. France
> thus enjoyed a ratio of one soldier to 225 civilians whilst England
> had one soldier to every 275, not a remarkable variation. The
> English population was far less widely spread than that of France,
> with the bulk living south of the river Trent and the great majority
> of these living in London, the south east and the West Country.
> Military coercion in England would have proved difficult and the
> army might, ultimately, have proved to be too small, but a policy

which aimed in that direction cannot, on these grounds, be dismissed as a bizarre dream. Because of the abbreviation of his tenure of office, it is only possible to catch glimpses of the policies which James might later have developed if he had been awarded a full span of years. These fleeting insights offer something very positive in the military field: the officer corps was reformed, the army was retrained, the whole military organization was made increasingly dependent on the king and it was often employed for military purposes. (Childs, 1980, pp.103–4)

The Declaration of Rights made the maintenance of a standing army in peacetime illegal without the consent of parliament. The Mutiny Act of 1689, which provided for speedy court martials for military personnel in cases of desertion, mutiny or sedition, was an attempt by parliament to enforce the army's loyalty to the revolutionary settlement in the peculiar circumstances of the Glorious Revolution. On occasions some Whig historians have been tempted to see this Act as rather more significant with parliament establishing authority over the army and, by making it a piece of legislation requiring annual renewal, ensuring the monarch's dependence on parliament. In fact, the initial Mutiny Act was only to last six months and the constitutional position of the army was unchanged; it remained under the sole command of the monarch – commissions, for example, came from the king, not parliament – and there were occasions during William's reign when the annual renewal of the Mutiny Act was allowed to slip.

The fear of how a standing army might be deployed continued during William's reign and, indeed, throughout the eighteenth century. Following the peace of 1697, parliament insisted on reducing William's army, and while expense was as much the reason as the old fears, it was the latter which constituted the most potent arguments. The king made no public complaint, but resorted to subterfuge to ensure that his best men were kept in the ranks and to endeavour to maintain higher numbers than parliament wished: in particular, he sought to disband newly raised units which had only seen garrison duty at home and replace them with his battle-hardened regiments from Flanders; he hoped also that some regiments could be 'lost' in Ireland – and given the accounting methods of the day this was not unrealistic.

Key developments in naval warfare went back to the second quarter of the century with the launching of three-deck battleships – *Couronne* in France in 1632, *Sovereign of the Seas* in England five years later; these ships, with their crews of 600 to 800 men, set the pattern for the sailing gunplatforms which fought the great naval battles through until Nelson's day. Yet the crucial years of naval expansion came in the last third of the century. The French navy was significantly developed under Colbert. His Forest Code of 1669 was designed to ensure a good supply of oak for battleships; subsequent ministers tightened up the code and in 1700 the navy was empowered to conduct a census of private forests near coasts and rivers marking out trees for naval use. In 1671 he established *conseils de construction* at the naval arsenals of Brest, Rochefort and Toulon to consider the best design for warships based on studies of how ships performed at sea. By the end of the century French warships were considered to be the best vessels on the seas. The English fleet was expanded initially because of the conflicts with the Dutch – and I use the

Figure 34
The Sovereign of the Seas.
(Mansell Collection)

word English advisedly since its supply was voted by the English parliament and it was paid for by English taxpayers, and while Scots and Irish seamen served on the ships, their countries were not formally involved with its organization. Royal forests in England were enclosed and replanted specifically with the interests of the navy in mind, but there was no attempt to reserve, and compulsorarily cut the trees of private landowners as in France. Private landowners did replant with naval demands in mind, but primarily with an eye to the profits which sales to the navy would bring. In both countries naval administration was overhauled and improved and a cadre of long-serving, able bureaucrats made their mark; most notable of these in England was the libidinous diarist Samuel Pepys (1633–1703), Clerk of the Acts from 1660 to 1673, then Admiralty Secretary from 1673 to 1679 and again from 1684 to 1690.

In 1688–9 the English and French navies were roughly balanced, with the Dutch only slightly smaller (see Table 1). But during the period 1689 to 1714 England gradually staked its claim to being the dominant sea power of Europe. The English parliament did not regard a standing navy as a potential threat to liberty like a standing army. The navy of the Tudors and the early Stuarts was, 'an occasional and motley body' provided 'by the monarch and certain nobles and merchants' (Kennedy, 1976, p.66). Increasingly, however, and especially after the Restoration, the navy became a national body financed by parliament with an enormous infrastructure of administration and logistics, notably in the great dockyards along the Thames, the Medway and the Channel. The navy became, at the same time, an instrument of commercial policy protecting the overseas interests of merchants, still often private monopolies operating under royal charters, and relieving them of the need to hire ships in their own defence.

Table 1: The principal battle fleets of Europe 1688–9

Rate*	Dutch	English	French
1st (90–100 guns)	4	9	13
2nd (80–90 guns)	4	11	20
3rd (70–80 guns)	9	39	40
4th (60–70 guns)	20	41	20
50–60 guns	16	–	–
40–50 guns	16	–	–
Frigates	19	8	38
Others#	14	65	90

*Only the first four rates of ship are properly construed as line-of-battle ships. The term ship-of-the-line dates from the late seventeenth century when the naval battle tactics meant that the old *mêlée* was replaced by ships sailing into action in line ahead. This kind of tactic required hardy ships, to withstand the battering of enemy broadsides as the lines joined in battle; efficient signalling systems, so that admirals could maintain command and authority over their line; and discipline in manoeuvre. The ship-of-the-line was one big enough to participate in such an action; the smaller warships and frigates were for reconnaissance and convoy duty.
Includes fireships, bomb vessels, and the 36 galleys which the French still had in the Mediterranean.

(*Source:* Adapted from Ehrman, J. (1953), *The Navy in the War of William III, 1689–1697*, Cambridge University Press, p.4)

But in spite of England's growing dominance at sea, for most of William III's wars against Louis XIV a similar stalemate to that on land seemed to be developing at sea, particularly as the two powers began to pursue different kinds of naval policy.

Exercise   Read *Anthology*, III.41 and answer the following questions.

1   What policy is Vauban advocating here?

2   What are his reasons for this policy?

3   What does he hope the outcome will be?

Discussion   I would expect you to have noted the following:

1   Vauban proposes that the naval side of the war against England and Holland should concentrate on privateering.

2   He considers the English and the Dutch to be the principal enemies of France; their strength is based on trade, and the best way of undermining that strength is therefore to strike at their commerce.

3   His principal hope is that a privateering war will cause the English and Dutch to make peace on terms far more favourable to France than would otherwise have been the case; in addition he sees a privateering campaign as reducing Louis XIV's expenses (as the privateers will not be funded and equipped by the king), increasing the pool of competent seamen on whom he can call, and bringing benefit to France from the goods seized by the raiders.

In fact, even before Vauban's memorandum, following their defeat at La Hogue (1692), the French had consciously opted to moth-ball many of their larger battleships and to concentrate on privateering. Swift 32-gun frigates began raiding from heavily fortified French ports like St Malo and Dunkirk; between 1689 and 1697, these captured some 4000 enemy vessels, mainly merchantmen. The ships were armed and equipped by private syndicates seeking high profits from the sale of captured cargoes and captured ships. These syndicates offered opportunities to business-men who were suffering from the economic dislocation of Louis's wars; some of them also included courtiers and even ministers; some of the privateer ships were leased from the king. The campaign did produce concern and calls for peace among merchant circles in both England and Holland, though it did not cripple their trade quite as Vauban had hoped. It also produced opportunities for some courageous and skilled seamen, of whom Jean Bart of Dunkirk was the most celebrated. During the famine of 1694 several of the privateer captains, notably Bart, success-fully brought grain supplies from Scandinavia through the North Sea avoiding, or defeating, the Anglo-Dutch squadrons which sought to inter-cept them.

Figure 35
Battle of La Hogue, 1692.
(Mansell Collection)

The men

The wars from 1689 to 1714 witnessed enormous demands for men. Louis XIV's army increased, for example, from 273,000 in 1691 to 395,000 five years later. William III called for 50,000 British soldiers and 22,000 sailors in 1689 and 66,000 soldiers and 48,500 sailors in 1695. But there are problems with such bald statistics. First and foremost, while the armies and navies were increasingly becoming professional and tied to a national monarch, they still contained a large number of foreign troops. Perhaps as many as three-quarters of Louis's wartime armies were made up of foreigners, often in complete foreign regiments. The point is made clearly in the fact that, alongside his demand for 50,000 British soldiers in 1689, William III also proposed to deploy 15,000 Dutch and 5,600 Danes financed by the English parliament. Louis XIV had regiments of Irishmen fighting under his flags against William (though his 'Irish' regiments were never wholly Irish). William had three regiments of 'Huguenots' in his British army – and again the inverted comas are used deliberately since some of the Huguenots were deserters from the French army, and Catholics. (In fact the word 'Huguenots' was commonly used in the seventeenth century to denote anyone who was French; it only acquired the specific meaning of French *Protestant* towards the end of the century.) Foreign ships, stopped on the high seas for insulting a flag or suspected of carrying contraband, might find members of their crew pressed into service by a boarding party; William's court and the Admiralty received constant complaints, particularly from Denmark and Sweden, over such actions.

Army recruits were expected to be volunteers who enlisted for the bounty paid them. Generally it was easier to find men in periods of dearth and economic hardship; as one French officer commented in 1709:

> The recruits who come to us are wiry men, accustomed to fatigue, who are forced to enlist because of the misery in the countryside; in a way you could say that the misfortunes of the people has been the safeguard of the kingdom. (quoted in Girard, 1921, p.72)

Of course, such safeguarding of the kingdom could lead to more misfortunes for the people as breadwinners, in the shape of fathers or fit strong sons, taken, sometimes permanently, from their families. Bounties had to be higher in seed-time and harvest time to attract men, but most recruiting was done in the winter months when the life of the poor was generally at its hardest and when the attraction of a warm uniform, shoes and money in the pocket must have been at its strongest. But it was not only because recruits were thought most likely to come forward during the winter that recruiting was then generally at its peak. Armies went into winter quarters, usually from October to April, since it was difficult to campaign when roads were impassable because of mud and when there was no fresh forage for horses; winter was therefore the period when small parties of perhaps an officer, a sergeant or two, some privates and a drummer could be spared. There was no conscription for the line armies, but in Scotland, during the 1690s, a system of quotas was tried to raise soldiers, first by a Privy Council ruling (1693–4), then by an act of the Scottish parliament (1696); each town and shire was given a specific number of men to produce, or else had to pay a fine. In both the British Isles and France there was widespread coercion and trickery in recruiting. It was also common for local magistrates to 'recruit' petty offenders and sturdy vagrants. In England, in 1704, when the need for soldiers was desperate, an act of parliament specifically authorized the forcible recruitment of able-bodied men without a lawful calling or visible means of support, but this legislation was probably sanctioning behaviour already in existence. Louis XIV disliked the idea of recruiting his soldiers from gaols. 'The obligation to serve the king', he wrote in 1705, 'has never been, and will never be, a punishment; it has never been declared or characterized as such' (quoted in Girard, 1921, p. 140). He stressed that men recruited from prisons should be considered as having received a pardon and a commutation of their sentence; but to the men involved, the finer points of Louis's reasoning were irrelevant.

A form of conscription did exist for the French navy. Between 1668 and 1673 Colbert established the *Inscription Maritime*. This required the registration of all seamen and fishermen; they were divided into classes which were required for service every fourth year or, in the case of Rochefort and Toulon, every third year. It was not intended that the rotation should work in wartime, but efforts were made to ensure that during a war deserving crews were rewarded and tired ones were refreshed. As a means of maintaining men's loyalty, and reducing the potential for the number of poor on the roads, the system provided for part of a man's pay to be given to his family. The flight of Huguenots following the revocation of the Edict of Nantes had a deleterious effect on the *Inscription*; 59,500 men were registered in 1686, but four years later the numbers had fallen to 55,800. There was also a decline in the efficiency of the system when, in keeping with the practices developed elsewhere in the bureaucracy to find money for his treasury, in 1704 Louis made the administrative offices in the system venal.

There were concerns about manning the royal navy for much of the period and an attempt was made to establish a Manning Register in England in 1696 somewhat on the lines of the French system. However, the English register was voluntary; and while the men on it were promised £2 a year retainer, by 1700 less than 20,000 were registered and less than a third seem to have been able-seamen. There were also abuses; register certificates were loaned or sold to enable men to escape the press gangs. Volunteers did come forward for the navy (again, as with the army, there were bounties for volunteers), but the attractions of the merchant service were generally greater: pay on a merchant ship was better, and more likely to be given at the end of the voyage; seamen on merchant ships were able to push up their wages in wartime, partly because of the dangers from French privateers, partly because of the crews being reduced by navy recruitment. Probably a majority of the men who served in the fleet during William's and Anne's wars were press-ganged, either by the gang of a land-based recruiting officer conducting a press in the seafarers' districts, or by the gang from a warship coming ashore or the siezure of men from a merchantman on the high seas. The press-gang was extremely unpopular, its appearance could provoke rioting and sometimes, this disorder was condoned by local officials; yet the methods of recruiting men for the royal navy seem to have been generally more effective, providing men in greater numbers than France's *Inscription*.

There is an interesting paradox here. After the Glorious Revolution especially, Englishmen of all social classes boasted of being 'free-born' and contrasted themselves favourably with their continental neighbours, especially the French, who were the subjects of an absolutist monarch and 'popery'. Yet in England recruitment by the press gang for the navy and, sometimes also for the army was more brutal and oppressive than that in France where the large build-up of men was achieved almost entirely by volunteering, albeit occasionally with pressure and/or trickery.

So far we have only looked at the rank and file, we need now to turn to the officers.

Exercise   Turn to *Anthology*, III.42, this is an extract from the lengthy memoirs of the duc de Saint-Simon, a French soldier and diplomat. You have already come across these memoirs which detail the theatre of the court at Versailles. During his lifetime Saint-Simon was known for his ardent desire to restore what he considered to be the nobility's loss of power to state bureaucrats (see Briggs, pp.163, 207). Read the document now, and answer the following questions.

1   What is Saint-Simon's complaint here?

2   What reasons does he give to justify his promotion?

3   Given the non-military reasons which Saint-Simon uses to stress the wrong done to him, can you see any potential for friction within the armies?

Discussion   1   Saint-Simon is angry first at his regiment being disbanded on the Peace of Ryswick with himself being given nothing to do, and second, and more important, at being passed over for promotion when war began again.

2   He notes the fact that he had served with distinction in four campaigns; he also stresses his birth, his dignity, and that of his close relations.

3   Clearly there could be problems if individuals were going to try to insist on social rank, rather than ability and long service for promotion; there might also be difficulties within regiments if officers were going to insist on the significance of their social rank and their social connections.

Figure 36
Louis, Duc de Saint-Simon, engraving by Mariage after Van Loo. (Mansell Collection)

Saint-Simon was always a stickler for the importance of social rank; as a junior officer he instigated an action against his commanding general on a point of precedence. The problem was that professional armies were emerging during the period, and professional armies required professional officers; yet the societies which supported these armies were divided by social ranks emanating from the old feudal division of society when the nobility and the gentry were largely a military caste. Many men like Saint-Simon, from the old feudal nobility – the *noblesse d'épée* – still saw military service for the king as their calling. This idea was fostered by Louis XIV, who developed a lavish household corps – the *maison du roi* – amounting to some 8500 men with some regiments, like the Musketeers, full of noblemen seeking advancement (note that Saint-Simon describes both his father-in-law and his father-in-law's brother as officers in the royal bodyguard, as well as holding other ranks). But Louis's demand for soldiers, and the increasing need to have professionals in command, meant that men from a lower part of the social hierarchy were promoted; some bourgeois even began to make it into the élite regiments of the *maison du roi*. Furthermore given the cost of serving as an officer, and the usual need to purchase the next rank on the ladder, Louis gave officers grants or pensions for good service which enabled some to advance higher in the officer ranks than might otherwise have been the case. While the social divisions were less marked in England, similar problems existed. Immediately after the defeat of Monmouth, the duke of Albemarle resigned from the army because the earl of Feversham and Lord Churchill had been promoted major-general over his head; and the following year the duke of Norfolk resigned 'considering it to be against his honour to be obliged to receive the commands of him of less dignity than himself' (quoted in Childs, 1980, p.46). William III considered war to be the profession of the monarch, and he also developed his household troops. Officers in his Guard regiments were ranked higher than those in the line regiments and generally got the senior promotions later in their career.

Whatever the squabbling about dignity and precedence, the overwhelming majority of officers continued to be drawn from the nobility and the gentry. But professionalism was also increasingly having an impact, and army officers were becoming an interest group as well as belonging to an existing social group. The end of the Nine Years' War, saw the implementation of half-pay for many of the officers of disbanded regiments; this could serve as a pension for the old and disabled, but it also held professionals in readiness for the next war. Equally important (and in parallel with the sale of other government posts as discussed in Unit 1), officers developed a proprietorial interest given the value of their commissions. A commission might be the result of a lifetime's saving. Moving up the ranks invariably required finding extra money for the purchase of a new commission; the sale of the old, lower rank could only provide a part of the new cost. The sale of a commission on a man's death also had a value; it might provide his widow's pension. A military career still provided impoverished young gentlemen of good family with the means of making a mark in the world, and perhaps even a fortune. The very end of our period saw the beginning of a considerable influx of young Scottish gentlemen into the English (now, perhaps more accurately, the British) army. Scotland was too poor to maintain them; the army offered adventure, and the chance of honour and wealth.

The situation was rather different in the navy. There was not so great a division between officers holding commissions and warrant officers here. A first rate man-of-war required about 800 men to crew her. At the top of such a ship's hierarchy was the captain and two or three lieutenants; these were the commissioned officers who commanded. But immediately below them were skilled men without whom the ship could not function and who served with royal warrants, rather than commissions; these men included the master (who actually sailed the ship), the boatswain, the carpenter, the gunner, the purser, the surgeon, the chaplain. These men had their assistants – the petty officers; after these came the able-seamen, and finally the ordinary seamen, and landsmen.

Again, social divisions seem to have been drawn more sharply in the French navy; though Colbert introduced the first systematic training for officers when he created a series of naval colleges in 1669. In England an examination was introduced for aspiring lieutenants in 1677; and no man could take this examination before the age of twenty and without having served two years at sea, one as a volunteer and one as a midshipman. Even so the English navy did witness rivalry between gentlemen and 'tarpaulins', as officers promoted from the warrant class were termed. On several occasions in his diaries Pepys described the anxieties which he and other officials felt over the problem. Thus, in December 1666, he recorded Sir William Batten, the Surveyor of the Navy, reporting gloomily 'that the gentlemen do give out that in two or three years a Tarpaulin shall not dare to look after being better than a Boatswain' (Bell, 1972, p.409).

Drawing on Pepys's descriptions many historians have tended to describe the navy of the Restoration through to William's wars as riven with dissension between increasingly dominant gentlemen and rough, tough, brave 'tarpaulins'. This led the most recent historian of the issue to pose 'one crucial question':

> If the gentlemen captains were really so bad, and really so dominant numerically, how did the royal navy manage to hold its own in two wars with arguably the best-commanded naval force of the age, the Dutch fleet, and manage in 1692 decisively to defeat the best-designed naval force, Louis XIV's new fleet? (Davies, 1991, pp.34–5)

Davies's balanced analysis shows that the divisions were generally not as serious, and rather more complex than the traditional view would suggest. Up to, and indeed during the second Dutch War, the division in the navy was largely a political one: the 'tarpaulins' were the old Interregnum officers, whom some of the newly appointed gentlemen officers found suspect. Subsequently the issue became one involving the great naval patrons of the day; some supported Pepys's interpretation of the disobedient, proud gentlemen, while others did not. In fact, there was often very little social difference between gentlemen and 'tarpaulins'; and as you might expect, there were good and bad seamen among both groups.

Again, there is an interesting Anglo-French contrast here. While French centralization is commonly contrasted with the situation in England, and while throughout this unit I have noted the increasing centralization of the French army, it is probably the case that, in contrast with the French army, the royal navy towards the end of the seventeenth century was more centralized, more bureaucratic and, in the long run, more efficient.

Auxiliary forces

In the section on 'Armies and navies' (above) you read something of the debate over a standing army in James II's reign. You also learned that James specifically preferred a standing army to the militia.

The militia was re-established by legislation between 1661 and 1663. It was a territorial force; officered by the gentry of a county, and with its rank and file balloted from the men of property in the county. In fact a large number of the rank and file were substitutes hired by the better off who had been balloted. The militias were expected to carry out four days' training each year in regiments, and to meet for two days, four times a year in their companies. They could be called out for much longer periods in an emergency. In theory the force amounted to some 6000 horse and 84,000 foot.

Exercise Given the lack of a standing army and the political situation at the beginning of the Restoration, what tasks do you suppose the militias could have been given by Charles II and his ministers?

Discussion   You may well have noted that the militias could be used as a police force
to keep an eye on, and intimidate potential troublemakers, and to search
for arms.

This is precisely what happened. As one historian has put it:

> Until the outbreak of the second Dutch War, the militia officer was
> part soldier, part policeman, and part secret serviceman: breaking
> up religious meetings, constantly searching for arms and suspicious
> persons, monitoring the post and watching the highways in an ever
> vigilant campaign to prevent the possibility of concerted republican
> action. (Norrey, 1988, p.792)

The performance of the militias was variable. The London Trained Bands
were rather similar bodies and were probably the most efficient and
effective. They remained loyal to Charles II (unlike their predecessors'
behaviour towards his father), notably patrolling the city against Fifth
Monarchy Men in 1662 and during the Exclusion Crisis. The Scottish militias were regarded as particularly competent, and there were concerns
that they could be marched into England to do the king's will. In
England large numbers of men turned out to face potential Dutch landings. But there were also counties where the lieutenancy made the militia
a low priority and where the regiments and companies were rarely
mustered even for their statutory annual training. Among the rank and
file there could be reluctance to turn out because of the loss of pay which
training entailed; while men were paid for their actual training, they were
not paid for the time (perhaps as much as a day or so), travelling to and
from their muster points. Some officers were concerned that their orders
in the early years of the Restoration left them open to litigation from
their victims, and legislation had to be passed to indemnify them; indem-
nified or not, there remained those who had little stomach for such
activity.

Much of this qualifies somewhat the notion of the militia as preferable to a standing army because it could not be used in an oppressive
way. But what of James II's criticism of the militias during Monmouth's
Rebellion?

Exercise   Turning back to the parliamentary debate reported in *Anthology*, III.39;
was there agreement with James's assessment of the role of the militias
during Monmouth's Rebellion?

Discussion   No. There were members who spoke up for the militia; both Sir Thomas
Clarges and Sir Hugh Cholmondley considered that it was useful during
the rebellion. Of course they may have been making the most of the
militias' behaviour in an attempt to ensure that no standing army was
established.

The consensus among historians seems to be that, in general, the county militias performed poorly during the rebellion: the Dorsets failed to oppose Monmouth's landing and withdrew into Bridport, where they remained; some of the Somersets fled before Monmouth's army, while two companies joined him. Yet it was probably significant to the campaign that the counter-marching of militias along their county boundaries prevented Monmouth from outflanking and avoiding the regular army under Feversham, while the militias' rapid reoccupation of places vacated by Monmouth, prevented the rebellion from seriously interrupting royal authority for long. It is also worth pointing out that Monmouth was captured by a patrol of the Sussex militia.

Monmouth's Rebellion confirmed James's preference for a standing army; the militia was increasingly ignored. His reorganization of the county lieutenancies involved the appointment of Catholics as lord lieutenant in 16 counties and as deputy lieutenants in about a third of the posts. Changing control at the top of the lieutenancies led to a further decline in the efficiency of the militias. James called on them for support against William, but received little. Subsequently some militia regiments were called out during emergencies in both William's and Anne's wars, notably the Norfolks in 1694 and 1697 because of the threat from French privateers. But the force generally was allowed to decay. There was no provision for a Scottish militia in the Act of Union and, in 1708, probably because of concerns about the influence of Jacobites in Scottish local government, Queen Anne vetoed a bill to create one – the last use of the royal veto in Britain.

The urban militia (*milice bourgeois*) of French towns dated back to the middle ages. These were men of property who were expected to turn out to defend their towns from enemy attack; they could also be used as a form of police force to patrol the streets in time of internal disorder or any other particular emergency. These militias were generally moribund by the late seventeenth century, though they might be brought back to life temporarily by a forceful military governor or when townsmen feared for their property and livelihood. There were a few other territorial militias in France during the third quarter of the century, notably in Béarn, Dauphiné, *les boulonoises* around Boulogne and the *miquelets* of Roussillon; these were corps raised in, and maintained for the defence of, their localities. In 1688, however, the demand for men to fight Louis XIV's wars was such that a new militia (*milice*) was organized to provide an auxiliary for the army.

Exercise   Turn to *Anthology*, III.43, read it, and answer the following questions:

1   How was the *milice* recruited?

2   What seems to have been the popular attitude to this force?

Discussion   1   The *milice* was recruited by ballot of the unmarried men in the parishes.

2   The service appears to have been extremely unpopular. Men employed a variety of stratagems to avoid the ballot, from running

away to getting married. Of those who were recruited, some died on the march to their regiments, while others deserted when the chance arose.

The provincial *intendants* were responsible for the overall supervision of *milice* recruitment and, depending on the military situation, different numbers were called each year: in 1688, the king demanded 23,800, and increased it from 38,050 in 1689 to 57,950 in 1690. The demands hit the *généralités* unequally. Originally the men were selected from the unmarried aged between twenty and forty, by a community vote (a useful way of getting rid of undesirables); the ballot was introduced in 1691, and twelve years later married men were also liable. *Miliciens* were to be supported, armed and equipped by their local communities. In theory the men were expected to serve for two years and were to return home when the army went into winter quarters. The *milice* were originally intended to act as second line troops, but from 1693 some were deployed in frontier regions in Catalonia, Flanders and Piedmont; and, after the defeats in northern Italy in 1701, some were used to fill the gaps in line regiments. Probably recruits to the *milice* saw little difference between the organization into which they were balloted and the line army. The scale of the *milice's* unpopularity may be judged by the enormous desertion rate. Overall figures are difficult to come by, but one example is instructive: between 17 March and 9 May 1705 some 13,929 *miliciens* were marched to Lyon as replacements for losses incurred by the army in Italy; some 3071 men (22 %) deserted while on the march.

You may have found it curious that the priest should say that militiamen died 'in great numbers' marching to join their regiments, alternatively you may have thought he was exaggerating, or that the deaths were the result of the physical weakness of the recruits. However, military service brought men from relatively remote areas into contact with diseases that their bodies had not met before and to which, in consequence, they had little or no immunity. Possibly also, the priest was referring, indirectly, to what became known in the French army as *nostalgie*. This was an acute form of what can best be described as home-sickness. It was recognized as a problem among peasant recruits in eighteenth-century armies. What it meant in practice was that young men, torn from their roots, with little understanding of the world outside their native village, could, if wounded or taken sick – even when the wound or sickness was slight – simply pine and die.

The army at home

The obvious use of the army is, of course, to fight foreign wars, but there was a variety of occasions during the second half of the seventeenth century when the troops of the French and British kings were deployed at home. There was civil war and rebellion which necessitated military intervention; there was also coercion. Louis XIV used his soldiers to enforce the Edict of Nantes, and he was compelled to withdraw men from the battlefronts to fight the *Camisards*. Charles II used his militiamen to harass and intimidate opponents. James II had to deploy militia and regular troops against Monmouth and Argyll; William's armies fought Jacobites in Ireland and Scotland. The quartering of troops on troublesome subjects as a punishment was practised in both countries, notably in France during the persecution of the Huguenots and in England following Monmouth's Rebellion. (Remember too Edward Seymour's complaint about the quartering of the army in private houses during the debate on James II's request for money for a standing army. Seymour appears to have been protesting here about instances where troops were quartered in private houses simply because there was no where else to put them.)

With little in the way of police forces in either France or the British Isles, troops were also used to suppress the less serious disorders resulting from food shortages or the enclosure of common land. In Britain troops were also used in support of the revenue, notably against smugglers; in France, in contrast, there was a special military police employed by the tax farms (see 'Footing the bill', below).

But troops were also a threat to public order, and the problem could become acute in wartime when marching regiments moved through a district, or when the numbers were considerably augmented in a garrison town. In 1668 the *intendant* of Burgundy received some 1800 complaints concerning the behaviour of the army bound for the conquest of Franche-Comté. Fifteen years later Louvois wrote to the *intendant* of Dauphiné to the effect that he should never attempt to negotiate with disorderly troops but that he should severely punish the first who offended, and 'if this should be one of the officers, it would be necessary in this case to put him in prison; and if it was a soldier or a dragoon, his Majesty desired that the man should be hanged' (quoted in Babeau, 1894, vol.2, p.120). In England, Portsmouth, a naval as well as an army base, suffered particularly and in May 1689 the local municipal authorities and the principal citizens petitioned for redress because of the problems created by:

> ... the soldiers left behind their colours, by their wives and children when they die or march, by the debts they contract beyond their pay, but particularly by the great disorders lately committed by the Irish, who not only made themselves masters of the houses by free quartering but threatened to destroy the petitioners which it is believed they would have done. (quoted in Beloff, 1938, p.112)

But Irishmen were not the only soldiers to create problems. Generally soldiers in both the British Isles and France were young men, they wore their bayonets and swords as part of their uniform, and once they had a few drinks inside them (though sometimes too, when they were sober) they were often as much a threat to their king's loyal subjects as they were to his enemies. In France special companies of military police, the *maréchaussée*, had been established during the sixteenth century in the different provinces to keep the king's troops in check. These policemen acquired other duties under Louis XIV; a royal ordinance of 1670 in particular gave them police authority over a variety of non-military offenders in the provinces. In Paris the problem of armed soldiers marauding in the streets after dark was one of the reasons prompting the creation of a new civilian officer, the *Lieutenant général de police de Paris*, in 1667. In England no separate policing bodies were developed to control troublesome soldiers; nor does anyone appear to have suggested such bodies, which may, in part at least, be because of the general English hostility to standing bodies of military.

Exercise   Now read *Anthology*, III.44 and answer the following questions.

1   What problem does de Radiolles identify here?

2   What seems to be the scale of the problem?

3   In which month did de Radiolles write the letter, and can you think of any reason why the problem might be worse then?

Discussion   1   De Radiolles reported that troops are participating in the smuggling of salt.

2   From the description of troops openly flouting authority the problem appears very serious and de Radiolles considered that it was getting worse.

3   The letter was written in January, which was outside the campaigning season, the troops were therefore in winter quarters and, arguably, bored with nothing much to do except seize the opportunity for making some extra money.

(In France the years of economic crisis brought about by Louis XIV's final wars and the succession of bad harvests fostered widespread smuggling. The smuggling bands drew on deserters from the armies and were often organized on a military footing; but there were also instances, such as those described by de Radiolles, when smuggling became the prerogative of army regiments themselves while in winter quarters.)

Generally speaking, the problems of criminal and disorderly soldiers, and sailors, in both France and the British Isles appear to have become most acute when armies and navies were disbanded at the end of wars and when some of the newly discharged men opted for a life of brigandage and banditry rather than a return to civilian life; but the evidence is largely anecdotal and there has been no systematic survey of the extent to which discharged soldiers turned to crime.

The problem of crime and brigandage among disbanded sailors and soldiers brings us on to the problem of what happened to men at the end of the military service.

There was no fixed term for military service in either Britain or France. You may recall the earl of Ranelagh's statement to parliament in November 1685 (*Anthology*, III.39): 'a Soldier is a Trade'. As with other trades, it was for life. The situation was different for men with seafaring skills who, at the end of a war, could generally move from the battle fleet to the merchant marine or fishing fleets (where most of them had come from in the first place). As regular armies developed, so the problem of what should be done about men who were too old or sick for active service became more and more apparent. In France a policy was introduced in 1669 to retire the six oldest men in each company in each year; however Louis's desire for soldiers subsequently saw this number reduced to four (in 1679), to one (in 1682), and finally suspended for the duration of his wars. No similar policy was introduced in England, though it was noted in 1673 that many men in the two regiments of foot guards were no longer fit for service because of age and/or wounds. In some instances men were kept on the muster rolls without any requirement that they perform military duties simply as a recognition of their good, long service, and to save them from penury in civilian life. Unfit and disabled men who were discharged were commonly seen as indigents or as a burden on their families and whatever passed for a poor rate. An exception in France was the continuance of a medieval system whereby a few former soldiers were accepted into religious houses as oblates.

Louis XIV and Louvois sought to solve the problem by providing hospitals where old, infirm and crippled soldiers could be cared for, and where workshops for shoemaking and tailoring could be provided for those who could still work. Les Invalides was built in the mid-1670s. It was designed for between 1200 and 2000 men living and working under strict discipline and religious observation. The problem was that as Louis's wars continued, Les Invalides found itself having to house more than 3000 men; its workshops had to be closed to provide dormitories. Elsewhere in France municipalities balked at the expense of building similar institutions, as was initially intended, and old soldiers in the provinces were left with the old choices.

But if institutions similar to Les Invalides were not built elsewhere in France, as was noted in Unit 14, the idea was taken up in Britain. Monmouth visited Les Invalides shortly after it opened. He asked Louvois for a copy of the plans to show Charles II. Others, like the duke of Ormond, viceroy of Ireland, were impressed with the institution. Kilmainham Hospital in Dublin, was opened in 1681, and Chelsea Hospital, in London, three years later. Again, neither was big enough to take all the veterans, particularly after the wars of William and Anne, and while a modest system of pensions was also introduced, the ex-soldier indigent or vagabond remained a problem.

Footing the bill

States needed men to fight their wars, but they also needed money to pay those men, to arm, equip and feed them.

Exercise Table 2 gives you a rough comparison of the costs of the wars to England and France. On which country does the burden appear to have been heaviest?

Table 2 The English and French war efforts compared

	Population	Total spending (per head in brackets)
England and Wales	5.2m (c.1688)	£8.1m (£1.56) 1696–7 £10.2m (£1.96) 1709–10
France	19.0m (c.1700)	£13.79m (£0.73) 1698 £15.00m (£0.79) 1711

(*Source*: Adapted from Jones, D.W. (1988), *War and Economy in the Age of William III and Marlborough*, Basil Blackwell Ltd, p.29)

Discussion   You will have noted from the table that the war appears to have been a greater burden on England and Wales where the cost, on a smaller population, worked out at roughly twice as much per head.

Exercise   Read Briggs, bottom of p.146 to p.148, and pp.156–7, and Coward pp.450–7, and answer the following questions.

1   Briefly, what happened to French finances between 1660 and 1714?

2   Briefly, what happened to English finances between 1660 and 1714?

3   Which financial system was functioning better during this period, and why?

Discussion   I would expect your answers to be something like the following.

1   Colbert set the French fiscal system on an even keel and made it work. In particular he put a greater emphasis on indirect taxation which affected the privileged as well as the poor. However Louis XIV's wars led to a variety of abuses being introduced into the system and culminated, on the king's death, in virtual state bankruptcy.

2   England underwent a financial revolution during this period. A bigger and better treasury was developed, contributing to an increase in the scale and sophistication of both direct and indirect taxation. A new system of public credit was created, most notably with the Bank of England, whereby specific parliamentary taxation was earmarked to pay off loans and interest. The crown became more and more dependent on parliamentary taxation, and the royal debts were replaced by the National Debt. At the same time the principal direct tax, the Land Tax, was paid by the privileged and wealthy, yet it was administered in the localities by local men and not by state bureaucrats.

3   Overall the English financial system appears to have been functioning better than the French. Even though the burden of the war seems to have been greater on the English, it was not the English state which was bankrupt in 1714; on the contrary, there was confidence in the system and it was recognized that the state (no longer just the monarch) did not renege on debts.

The two exercises above demonstrate that the raw figures of a state's expenses have to be interrogated by an assessment of the fiscal efficiency (not to mention the potential wealth) of that state before serious judgements can be made about the financial impact of war. The question now arises – why, in comparison, was the French system so inefficient?

Qualifications and caveats have to be made when the annual income and expenditure of the governments of William and Anne are discussed by historians. However the figures have a degree of reliability and enable economic historians to draw conclusions about the respective significance of customs, excise, Land and Assessed Taxes, and borrowing at the end of the seventeenth and beginning of the eighteenth centuries.

For Louis XIV's France the situation is far more complex and historians find it difficult to assess the true amount of revenue collected annually and the level of the taxation burden on the population. There are several reasons for this.

One way of raising money in France was by the sale of offices. This has created a problem for historians in that part of the revenue collected in localities remained in the localities to pay some of the office-holders, and it is not clear how much. More serious for Louis, the practice was a two-edged sword. Although purchased offices brought in revenue, they generally included exemptions from certain direct taxes; thus they undermined the attempts to increase direct taxes and curtail the fiscal privileges of nobles and office-holders. An increase in direct taxation depleted the spending power of everyone, but especially the peasants and artisans who had much less in the first place; such a depletion meant that they had less to spend in, for example, their local *cabarets*, consequently the receipts from the indirect taxes on drink declined.

Indirect taxes, as you will recall from Units 1 and 6, were farmed out (literally) in France. The Company of Farmers General was a syndicate of financiers who leased from the king the right to collect the taxes on commodities in return for an annual fixed sum. Such taxes fell on salt (*gabelle*), tobacco, wine, cider and other alcoholic drinks, on gold and silverwork, leather work and so on (*aides*). The tax farmers paid their organization and made their profits from the amount which they collected in excess of the annual sum promised to the king. Since most of their records were destroyed in the Revolution it is difficult to estimate their overheads and profits. Colbert unified the tax farms in the 1660s ultimately creating a single organization. But Louis's wars undermined the system. During the 1690s the tax yields of the farmers plummeted; they began to borrow on their own credit and also loaned to the king at a high rate of interest; to keep them in business Louis had to compensate them for their lack of profits. In 1703 Louis's ministers found it difficult to negotiate a new lease with the farmers; six years later they refused a new lease entirely, and would not agree to another until 1714. In the meantime their bureaucracy continued to function, often with administrative advice and direction from the farmers themselves, but in the king's name.

Tax farming had its advantages: it guaranteed a monarch a fixed annual sum, regardless of the costs of collection; it deflected public hostility to taxation away from the monarch to the farmers. The unpopular police of the tax farmers – the *gabelous* – were, for example, no concern of the state and could not always rely on support from the state's own rural police, the *maréchaussée*. But tax farming also made the king and his government potentially subordinate to their creditors. The system existed in England, but was gradually phased out in the later years of Charles II and under James II. Some offices could be purchased in England, most obviously commissioned rank in the army; but such purchases did not bring other fiscal privileges. Perhaps the greatest single difference between English and French direct taxation was the fact that in England the principal direct tax was the Land Tax, which fell mainly on the ownership of land, and thus on those best able to pay. Moreover it was agreed by parliament, which was full of landowners, and its collection was administered locally, by local worthies, again largely landowners. In

France the nobility were exempt from the principal direct tax, the *taille*, which was imposed on assessed income in about 95 per cent of the kingdom and on land in the remainder. Thus while the overall burden may have been heavier in England, the system seemed more fair.

This description of how the taxation systems functioned in the two countries takes us back to one of the key comparisons in the course – the outcome of the respective English and French constitutional struggles during the seventeenth century. This issue is central to the debate about absolutism: it was discussed in Unit 12, but I want to return to it here in drawing this unit to a close.

The British monarch remained immensely powerful, yet his ability to raise taxes was lost to parliament; remember too how parliament kept a watchful eye on the monarch's army, especially in peacetime. In France indirect taxation was the result of the negotiations between the king's ministers and leading financiers. Direct taxation depended upon orders from the king's ministers to his bureaucrats in the provinces – though, of course there might have to be some further negotiations with the privileged members of provincial estates. No intermediary body could exert any pressure on the monarch regarding the size of his army in peacetime. Yet the differing constitutional relationships do not explain in themselves why the British financial system became more efficient; and what was to stop an absolute monarchy from reforming the taxation system root and branch, especially when the army could be relied upon to enforce the king's desires, when the kingdom appeared under threat during war, and when the financial system was recognised as being in a mess? In 1695 Pontchartrain introduced the *capitation* and in 1710 Desmarets introduced the *dixième*; both were direct taxes which fell on the wealthy and privileged as well as the poor. What, perhaps, was lacking in France was the political will to devise and to push through sweeping fiscal reforms and to face the fury which they could have provoked.

Conclusion

Tangentially this unit has raised several questions relating to the of the state and political systems in Britain and France towards the end of the seventeenth century. By way of a brief conclusion let me draw together some of these issues and encourage you to consider them as you develop your own views.

The British boasted of being 'free born' and possessing 'liberty' in contrast to their continental neighbours, and especially the French. Yet their government sanctioned a system of military, and particularly naval, recruitment which was more brutal and oppressive than that in France. The French are generally recognized as having a state far more centralized than that in the British Isles; their armed forces, especially their army, were manifestly becoming more centralized and bureaucratic, and were considered a model for others. Yet, for its royal navy, Britain appears to have developed an administration and bureaucracy more centralized and more efficient than any French structure. Furthermore, for all its administrative centralization the French state used private financial entrepreneurs to collect its taxes. Britain, in contrast, had a centralized, state-run taxation system which was generally regarded as more fair; and the British appear to have paid, per capita, more taxes than the French. How do all of these issues marry up with the traditional picture of French absolutism and the British contrast?

References

Babeau, A. (1894), *La province sur l'ancien régime*, 2 vols, Paris. (Reprinted AMS Press, New York, 1972.)

Beloff, M. (1938), *Public Order and Popular Disturbances, 1660–1714*, Oxford University Press, Oxford.

Childs, J. (1980), *The Army, James II, and the Glorious Revolution*, Manchester University Press, Manchester.

Davies, J.D. (1991), *Gentlemen and Tarpaulins: The Officers and Men of the Restoration Navy*, Clarendon Press, Oxford.

Ehrman, J. (1953), *The Navy in the War of William III, 1689–1697*, Cambridge University Press, Cambridge.

Girard, G. (1921), *Racolage et milice (1701– 1715)*, Plon, Paris.

Jones, D.W. (1988), *War and Economy in the Age of William III and Marlborough*, Basil Blackwell, Oxford.

Kennedy, P.M. (1976), *The Rise and Fall of British Naval Mastery*, Macmillan, London.

Latham, R. and Matthews, W. (eds) (1972), *The Diary of Samuel Pepys*, vol.VII, G. Bell, London.

Norrey, P.J. (1988), 'The Restoration Regime in Action: The Relationship between Central and Local Government in Dorset, Somerset and Wiltshire, 1669–78', *Historical Journal*, 31, pp.789–812.

Parker, G. (1988), *The Military Revolution: Military Innovation and the Rise of the West, 1500–1800*, Cambridge University Press, Cambridge.

Unit 16
Reviewing the course

*Prepared for the course team by
Anne Laurence*

Contents

Study timetable

Weeks of study	Texts	Video	AC	Set books
2	Offprints	Video 14 and various TV programmes and video extracts	AC2, section 8	Coward, Briggs

During the period of this unit you should also view again TV7 and 8.

Objectives

The objectives of this unit are that, by the end of the unit, you should:

1   be able to discuss the extent to which the power of the two monarchies was sustained or declined in the period 1685–1714;

2   understand how historians use different kinds of evidence to draw their conclusions;

3   understand what kinds of change had taken place in France and in the British Isles between 1620 and 1714, looking in particular at the role of the state, its form and functions, and at the relations between princes and peoples.

The unit should also help you prepare for the exam by revising the earlier parts of the course and by reviewing them in a comparative perspective.

Introduction

This unit is arranged in three parts. In the first part I shall offer a consideration of the events and developments which took place in France and the British Isles in the later seventeenth and early eighteenth centuries. In the second part I shall consider the types of evidence which we have used in the course. And in the third part I shall review the whole period 1620–1714 and consider what changes had taken place in the state and in relations between governors and governed during that time.

The final years, 1685–1714

In Units 11, 12, 13 and 15 we considered the history of the later years of Louis XIV's reign and the period in the British Isles after the Glorious Revolution of 1688 in the contexts of the development of resistance to the government, the development of absolutism, ideas which supported or opposed it, and the creation of a military machine. We have also seen something in Block 2 of social and religious developments in this period. You have read parts of Coward, pp.351–492 and Briggs, pp.144–205 which cover this period. You should now look back at these passages and make sure you understand the general developments discussed there.

John Miller (1987, p.211) claims that in 1685 the monarchies of France and England were at the zenith of their powers. In this first section of the unit I want to look at the extent to which in the years following, the monarchies of France and the British Isles might be seen to be somehow declining from this zenith. I also want to look at the impact of some changes of the later seventeenth century on ordinary people.

Monarchies

In his study of the *noblesse de robe* and the *noblesse d'epée*, the historian Franklin L. Ford argued that Louis XIV's regime was based upon 'the approval of a population which had turned from the anarchy of the Fronde to seek order as an absolute good' and where the notion of order was equated with 'every rank and every individual assigned a fixed place in relation to the crown' (Ford, 1965, pp.5–6). But by 1715 this essentially static system was crumbling, held chiefly in place by the survival of King Louis XIV himself. Ford's remarks show how difficult it is to differentiate between an assessment of Louis XIV's achievements and an assessment of the period as a whole. In part, this is the result of the king's extraordinarily long reign – 72 years – a period during which there was a republic and four reigns in the British Isles. Here, we are concerned with the last 30 years of Louis's reign and with the reigns of William and Mary and Anne. Let us consider first what Ford refers to as the approval of the population.

There were certainly challenges to Louis's government, but it is probably fair to say that in France there was no challenge to the institution of monarchy. Rather, there was opposition to policies (fiscal and military) which were central to his regime and latterly this was expressed as opposition to Louis XIV himself. In 1694, in a letter which Louis never saw, Fénelon wrote 'you have spent your entire life off the path of truth and justice, and consequently off the path of the Scriptures' (quoted in Campbell, 1993, p.148). This might have been a particularly explicit condemnation of the personal government, but most historians would agree that:

> The wars and royal policies were to stimulate an internal critique and virulent foreign propaganda, which undermined the stately facade to the extent that few were sorry to see the end of the reign. (Campbell, 1993, p.86)

Nevertheless, neither the critiques nor the propaganda fundamentally challenged Louis's vision of order.

In England, the Glorious Revolution demonstrated the nation's preference for the institution of monarchy. However, the consensus which had prevailed during the immediate crisis of the deposition of James II and the invitation to William III did not last long. Such issues as the standing army and the constant need for war finance soon aroused as vociferous an opposition as the early Stuart kings had faced. As we saw in Unit 13, there was a revival of interest in republicanism, less as an attack on the very institution of monarchy, than as a means of justifying limitations on its powers. There was, too, the natural reluctance of Tories and some members of the Anglican hierarchy to accept that James II, as a king by divine right, might be legitimately replaced by someone whose claim was validated by parliament rather than by hereditary descent.

For his whole reign, as we can see in the debate about the oath of allegiance, there was dispute about the nature of the king's claim. The previous phrasing of the oath of allegiance to the monarch contained the phrase 'right and lawful'. Only after the attempt to assassinate William in 1696 (and two years after the death of Queen Mary whose presence had been a salve to some Tory consciences) was the majority of the House of Commons prepared to undertake to uphold William as 'rightful and lawful' king. Only after Louis XIV's recognition in 1702 of James II's son as James III were all office-holders, churchmen, Nonconformist ministers, schoolmasters, college fellows and MPs required to take an oath of allegiance by which they acknowledged William as 'lawful and rightful' king (still not quite the same words as the old oath of allegiance) and abjured the claims of James III as Pretender. So, whilst it might be said that William had the approval of the people in England, it was somewhat qualified.

In Scotland and Ireland obvious support for the continuing claims of James II and his descendants was much stronger than it was in England. To gain the consent of the people in England, who after all had brought William over, was rather different from securing the approval of the people of Scotland and Ireland who were faced with a *fait accompli*. William took over the institutions of government in Scotland but how effective their capacity was to implement royal policy is uncertain, and there was strong support for James, both amongst those who believed in his unalterable claim and amongst Episcopalians who opposed the covenanting Presbyterians. By comparison with the support which James enjoyed in Ireland, however, Scotland was easily won over to William. In Ireland James had ruled with the approval of the Catholic majority, and William's assumption of the crown was followed by the lengthy period of suppression known as the Williamite wars. It is worth noting that the Presbyterians, whose numbers considerably increased in Ireland during the late seventeenth century and early eighteenth century, were excluded from public office since the penal laws were framed in such a way as to apply to dissenters. There was no Irish equivalent to the English Toleration Act of 1689.

Queen Anne reigned with the approval of the people in England, though at the back of everyone's mind was the problem of the succession. Many English Tories were uncertain about the prospect of a Hanoverian monarch. Protestant ascendancy governors in Ireland were convinced of the need for the Hanoverian succession, but the issue was much less clear-cut in Scotland. The removal of bishops from the Scottish Upper House and the abolition of the Lords of the Articles, the committee which managed the Scottish parliament, reduced the monarch's power to control parliamentary proceedings there.

Exercise   Looking back at Units 11 and 13 and the Offprints and using Coward and Briggs (consult the index and the date charts) make a note of any indications that the approval of the people was withheld from the monarchy of the two states after 1688. I am not going to set you specific pages to read because you have already read much of this material.

(It's an important skill to be able to sift what you read and locate relevant material.)

Discussion   In France you could have mentioned what Bill Purdue refers to in Unit 13 as the military-fiscal (or fiscal-military) state. In such a state, taxes are high to pay for the army, which then has to be used either to collect taxes from an unwilling population or to suppress tax revolts, such as that of the Tard-Avisés in Quercy in 1707. Briggs (p.148) refers to this as 'the classic extortion-coercion situation'.

You might have mentioned Protestants and Jansenists, though you need to think about what proportion of the population was involved. It may be that there were as many as a million Huguenots, of whom between 150,000 and 250,000 (between 15 and 25% of the Protestant population of France) emigrated. The Camisards' revolt in the Cévennes in 1702–5, was a violent popular reaction to the persecution of Protestants. Though Louis's persecution of the Jansenists was intense, it affected only a relatively small number of people, albeit people of considerable status and influence. It was never a mass movement in the way that Protestantism was. The resurgence of the Jansenist quarrel in Louis's final years antagonized a good many of the *noblesse de robe* and aroused public sympathy for the persecuted.

In England, the monarchy enjoyed the approval of much of the population in 1688–90. Just as Louis XIV had won support for bringing order after the chaos of the Frondes, William briefly basked in the warm afterglow of averting the popish threat. However, his attempts to champion Protestantism on a wider stage, by war in Europe, soon provoked antagonism to his war policies, in the country opposition of the early 1690s (Coward, p.374) and in the campaign against a standing army in 1697 (Coward, p.386).

It is difficult to know how far party rivalries and anxiety about the Protestant succession actually reflected approval for or disapproval of the monarchy. But there is no doubt that party propaganda used and exaggerated differences over a range of issues including the monarchy to score points over political rivals.

I asked you about the approval of the population for the monarchies of France and Britain, but in fact Franklin L. Ford (see p.149, above) was primarily concerned with the population's desire for order. To what extent did monarchs achieve this after the 1680s? Briggs (p.149) refers to 'a rising tide of criticism and hostility' to the government of France from the 1680s, but without specifying who was responsible. On pp.162–3 he suggests that lack of confidence in Louis's policies was increasingly discernible in criticism of the government rather than in the appearance of an identifiable opposition. There does not seem, except in certain specific instances, to have been a breakdown of order. There's even an implication that France was paralysed by its bureaucratic structures and over-regulation (Briggs p.158). The monarch had certainly quashed the claims of nobles and sovereign courts to challenge royal policy, but had done so by the use of traditional forms of patronage and by the expansion of the royal bureaucracy to an unprecedented size. Royal patronage was transferred from nobles and their provincial clienteles to ministerial networks of administrators. Louis's suppression of Protestantism was undoubtedly popular amongst the Catholic French population and removing Protestants disposed of an element of French society which offended against Louis's idea of order.

In general Louis was very effective in dispersing opposition at home. Quite the reverse seems to have been the case abroad. Briggs (p.150) makes the point that it was Louis XIV's style of aggression that encouraged European powers to ally with one another. He is very free with terms like 'megalomaniac' and 'egotistical' to explain Louis's behaviour. For Louis the enhancement of his personal reputation, the confirmation of *la gloire*, was in successful warfare. The European war had mixed effects upon William's domestic standing. On the one hand it confirmed parliament's power of the purse (Coward, p.379), but it also increased the monarch's control over the executive and massively enlarged the bureaucracy, a process that continued into Anne's reign (Coward, p.452).

Whilst warfare created a number of recognizably 'modern' institutions it still carried with it ancient ideas of nobility. Warfare was the means by which a man established his claims to be truly noble (in the moral as well as in the social sense). In his advice to his grandson in 1700 Louis wrote: 'If you are forced to make war, put yourself at the head of your armies' (Déon, 1991, p.95). In warfare we can see in their most distilled form the contradictions between the formation of new institutions and the cult of the king as a noble military leader. Both Louis and William exploited this cult to a considerable degree.

Video Exercise Watch Video 14 and consider whether you think that images which Louis XIV constructed for himself were qualitatively different from those made by contemporary British monarchs?

Discussion It was certainly to William's advantage that he was able to portray himself as a man of action, riding vigorously, often on a galloping horse. Louis, when shown on the battlefield, usually appears as a spectator in seventeenth-century dress. More often he is shown as a Roman general in some allegorical pose. Allegorical poses of William are most likely to stress his Protestantism; he did not need allegorical portrayals of his military successes.

Figure 37
Louis XIV shown as a Roman victor. *Portrait of Louis XIV, victorious at Maastricht by Pierre Mignard, 1673, oil on canvas, 304.8 cm. x 234 cm. Pinacoteca, Turin. Photo: Alinari.*

Figure 38
William III shown as a Roman victor*; an unusual depiction of William who more commonly appears in contemporary dress. William III, equestrian portrait by Sir Godfrey Kneller, 1701, oil on canvas, 439.4 cm. x 424.2 cm. Royal Collection © 1994 Her Majesty Queen Elizabeth II.*

Nevertheless, there is no doubt that the portrayals of the two kings derive from a common culture, especially in the use of classical gods and heroes and Roman emperors, a culture shared by most of the monarchs and nobles of western Europe and enhanced by their desire to emulate the French king and his court.

Despite these magnificent images, it is clear that the person of the king was a frail vessel for *la gloire*. Briggs is cynical about the later years of Louis's reign, suggesting public distrust of the symbols of monarchy so carefully constructed by and for Louis XIV. On p.150, for example, he refers to Louis's 'obsessive concern for the prestige of his dynasty'. Pierre Goubert writes of how in his final weeks of life 'useless brutality alternated with modes of elephantine subtlety' (Goubert, 1970, p.275). This tone is not peculiar to twentieth-century historians. In the 1690s the ambassador from Brandenburg referred to the king's 'naturally limited intelligence' and added that 'he is absolutely jealous for his own authority and unreasonably sensitive of any threat to it' (Campbell, 1993, pp.114–15). Lord Montagu referred to him as 'the vainest creature alive' (Campbell, p.119). And look at Illustration Book (Pl. 76) for William Makepeace Thackeray's brilliant summing up of Louis's reign from his Paris sketchbook of 1840, published with the comment 'You see at once, that majesty is made out of the wig, the high-heeled shoes, and cloak ... Thus do barbers and cobblers make the gods we worship' (Burke, 1992, frontispiece).

Princes

Perhaps one of the most striking changes to take place in France was the emasculation of the princes of the blood. Remember the terrible trouble caused to the French monarchy by the activities of Gaston d'Orléans, and of the various princes of Condé, especially the great Condé during the Fronde of the nobles? Contrast the role of the princes of the blood in the early part of the period with that of Louis XIV's brother, Philippe d'Orléans of whom little has been written in English.

Noblemen had become courtiers by the latter part of Louis's reign, their system of working through networks of clients in a provincial power-base taken over by royal administrators. But the provincial networks of the new administrators were built up gradually, using the power of the old nobility. By keeping great nobles tied up at court, their provincial clienteles withered and with them noble military power. Even noble households diminished in size. While domestic servants increased in number, the armed retainers who had been such an important feature of late medieval noble status, became increasingly insignificant. But this was only a minority of the nobles. Remember the thousands of nobles in Brittany alone, living in their manors quite divorced from the life of the court?

William III was welcomed by both houses of parliament and the negotiations which followed appeared to mark the triumph of the House of Commons. But the House of Lords was by no means emasculated. While the status of individual members had no equivalent to that of great nobles in France, the House of Lords was an extremely important body. Powerful politicians could expect to pass from the Commons to the Lords

and there to continue, or even enhance, their political influence. Most
senior ministers were in the Lords and a historian of the reign of Queen
Anne has argued that:

> ... the House of Lords was unquestionably supreme as a political
> forum throughout Queen Anne's reign ... There were periods in
> every one of Anne's parliaments when the Upper House manifestly
> rivalled the Lower in real political importance. (Holmes, 1967,
> p.383)

But to say this is not to say that the nobility as a caste held much power.
The House of Lords was more susceptible than the Commons to management by the court, not least because it had fewer members. In 1703 its
total membership, excluding Catholics, exiled peers and minors, was 161
of whom perhaps two-thirds were active, and the addition of the Scottish
peers did not increase the numbers by many. Far more of the administration of England and Wales was in the hands of commoners, as members
of the commissions of the peace, than was in the hands of peers and it
was the county gentry who made up the body of the House of Commons.
It is clear that the preservation of property rather than the preservation
of status was becoming the driving force of political activity.

The concept of nobility seems to have been losing its political force
in England and Wales after 1688, but this seems to have been much less
the case in Scotland. Nobles played an important political role in 1688. It
was Scottish noblemen who asked William to assume control of the
government until the estates could meet. Companies of volunteers led by
noblemen and inspired by the clergy ensured that the lowlands and the
towns were soon under William's control. He required the co-operation
of such magnates as the Dukes of Argyll, Atholl, Hamilton and Queens-
berry. But it was also aristocrats who led the resistance to William in the
Highlands and the strength of their opposition had the effect of bringing
the Highland clans into the orbit of European politics, instead of being a
geographically and culturally marginal group. The removal of the power
base to London in 1707 meant that Scottish aristocrats loyal to the revolution settlement had to go to London in search of fortune and political
favours. This opened the way for lairds, the equivalent of the English
gentry, to play a larger role in local government.

In Ireland, William, after the conclusion of the war in 1691, had
regarded the confiscated estates of James II's Catholic supporters as his
personal property to dispose of to those who had done him favours: his
generals, advisers, supporters and 'his intelligent, squint-eyed mistress',
Elizabeth Villiers (Simms, 1986, p.11). The English parliament believed
that these lands should be sold to defray the cost of subduing Ireland.
They cancelled William's personal grants and appointed trustees to
administer the confiscated estates, with no reference to the Irish parliament, which did not even meet over this period. Many Catholic nobles
lost their lands in this confiscation, though Catholic peers were not formally excluded from the House of Lords until 1716, nor Catholic free-
holders from the House of Commons until 1726. The continuing threat
of new Jacobite activity created, amongst the political nation, a Protestant
consensus loyal to the crown though the parliament at Westminster was
determined not to let William establish any kind of independent power
base in Ireland, resolving that Ireland was a 'dependent and subordinate
kingdom'.

Peoples

The French historian Pierre Goubert (1970, p.179) notes that from 1685 to 1688 good weather, large harvests and cheap grain alleviated the lot of ordinary people after a period of high taxation and poor harvests. But any benefit was soon dissipated by the effects of the nine years of indecisive war which accompanied Louis's *réunion* claims. One effect was that a much higher proportion of the population of France was taxed. The privileges of certain estates not to pay tax were undermined by such devices as *dons gratuits*, a kind of forced loan, and by the introduction in 1695 of a capitation tax from which there were no exemptions. There was also a severe trade depression. The effects of the war were exacerbated by the terrible famine in France of 1693–4 caused by an accumulation of factors: bad weather and poor harvests over several years afforded no chance of recovery. The former ambassador from Brandenburg, writing in the 1690s, commented on 'the misery of the poor people and the folk of the countryside, exhausted by the *tailles*, by the billeting of soldiers and by the *gabelles*' (Campbell, 1993, p.115). The tax demands depleted people's savings so they could not afford to pay for more expensive food in times of shortages, so you can see why in 1694 there were:

> … poor souls, weak from hunger and wretchedness and dying from want and lack of bread in the streets and squares, in the towns and countryside. (quoted in Goubert, 1970, p.216)

It was sights such as this which started to galvanize opposition to the king, as, for example, Fénelon's of 1695, 'your victories and conquests no longer delight … [your people] is full of bitterness and despair' (*Anthology*, III. 28). A brief period of respite was ended in 1701 by a terrible epidemic, possibly dysentery, possibly measles. Then war resumed, this time over the Spanish succession. An exceptionally severe winter ravaged the crops of 1710 almost before they had germinated, and poor harvests in 1712, 1713 and an epidemic of cattle disease in 1714 wrought further damage.

An important aspect of these wars was the sheer numbers of people involved. In the War of the League of Augsburg or Nine Years' War (1688–97), France armed and equipped 200,000 men and two fleets. In 1703 there were 300,000 men in arms for France. At Blenheim in 1704, some 30,000 soldiers from the French army were killed, captured or ran away. The depression of the years after 1710 created a supply of young men desperate for work and willing to serve in the army.

The French wars exacted a smaller personal toll from the British Isles. The inhabitants of these islands were, after all, merely one of the allies in the anti-French coalition. Nevertheless there were economic changes under way which affected the lives of many of those who lived in the countryside – the majority of the population. Landowners were consolidating their property. Noblemen who saw no future in politics turned their attention to agricultural improvement and to maximizing the return on their land. Lesser landowners found themselves in difficulties and the poorest country dwellers, increasingly deprived of land, were forced to work as day labourers. Everyone was affected by raised taxation and overseas commercial ventures were inhibited by the war.

In Scotland popular support for King James seems to have been connected with clan loyalties. New taxes for the war, dislocation of trade and the years of famine in Scotland (1696–1700) all took their toll. The administration of poor relief was inhibited by the chaos following the exclusion of Episcopalian ministers in many parishes. The Act of Union does not seem to have had much immediate impact upon ordinary people's lives, chiefly because such people had little contact with the institutions of central government. But it was clear that there was a reservoir of discontent, which overflowed in 1715.

Ireland was much involved in the War of the Spanish Succession, providing men and supplies for the English campaigns in Spain and northern Europe. It was also raided by French privateers and regarded with concern by the Protestant authorities as a possible source of sympathy for the French. And there was a succession of bad harvests. While the Protestant gentry became more assertive of their rights, the mass of the population was subjected to the penal laws, which were intended to emasculate Roman Catholics lest they rise again in support of James II and his successors. J.G. Simms contends that the laws were modelled on those passed against Catholics in England and had they been effectively implemented, Catholicism would not have stood much chance of surviving in Ireland. As it was:

> … the laws against clerics and religious observances were ineffectively and spasmodically administered, with the result that catholicism showed a remarkable power of survival and for much of the time was openly connived at. The laws affecting property were more stringently executed, so that most of those catholic families that owned land eventually became Protestant. Other catholics conformed in order to practise at the bar or to become solicitors. (Simms, 1986, p.16)

The laws were passed over the period 1695–1714 and involved the progressive removal of the personnel and institutions of Roman Catholicism and restrictions on the ownership and long-term occupation of land by Catholics. In 1697 all Catholic bishops and members of the regular orders were banished, a measure which had been held up until the influence of William's Catholic anti-French allies had diminished somewhat. Simms observes the paradox that in the very year that it was passed, Louis XIV recognized William as king in place of James.

Witchcraft revisited

Throughout the course we have seen a tendency for the state to extend its control over all social groups including the very poor. By the early eighteenth century the organs of the state in France and the British Isles were very much more effective than they had been in 1620.

Yet there was one area in which state control diminished most markedly. In France the majority of witch trials took place before 1640, but from the 1630s there had been a marked decline in the number of executions of witches tried in the jurisdiction of the *parlement* of Paris. The legal persecution of witches ceased in the 1670s when Louis XIV and Colbert intervened to stop a witch hunt in Normandy and the south west of France. A royal ordinance of 1682 reduced the crime of witchcraft to one of fraud (Briggs, p.205). In England, which had had about the same level of prosecutions as France, the last execution took place in 1685 and the last witch was tried at Hertford assizes in 1712. In Scotland the level of acquittals rose with the later outbreaks of witch persecution, and the last execution took place in 1706. The English acts against witchcraft were repealed in 1736 and a House of Lords amendment repealed the 1563 Scottish Act, creating in both countries a new offence which amounted to little more than fraud, punishable by a year's imprisonment.

How was it that a phenomenon which had caused a tremendous amount of disruption in small communities and consumed a good deal of time in the courts of England, Scotland and France simply disappeared? It is important to remember that the actual number of prosecutions was never large and that the number of successful prosecutions was even smaller.

Exercise Can you see any connection between the extension of state control over people's lives and the decline in witchcraft prosecutions?

Discussion It is tempting to answer that the extension of mechanisms of state control meant that the policing of small communities passed more to officials, to village *syndics*, to kirk sessions and to village constables, overseers of the poor and churchwardens, all answerable to a better developed administration of *intendants* and commissions of the peace. But do you remember from Unit 9 that one of the reasons I offered for the *rise* in witchcraft prosecutions was spread of uniform forms of religion and systems of justice? I mentioned the use of prosecutors in Scotland and France. Is it not, then, rather contradictory to see the decline as the product of the same thing? Or was it just that the government was so effective in its prosecuting policy that witches were eradicated?

If you actually looked back at Unit 9, you may also have noted that in France the higher the court to which witchcraft prosecutions were taken, the less likelihood there was of a verdict of guilty. Senior judges in the *parlement* of Paris became increasingly sceptical of the validity of witchcraft prosecutions. This scepticism seems to have extended beyond the region round Paris. In 1652 the Cromwellian commissioners in Edinburgh for want of proof dismissed 60 men and women who had been brought before them on various witchcraft-related charges. Everywhere it proved to be increasingly difficult to get law officers to pursue cases of witchcraft, and even if such cases got into the courts they were often dismissed without coming to trial. Robert Boyle's view expressed in 1677 (and quoted in Thomas, 1973, p.693), that 'We live in an age and place wherein all stories of witchcrafts, or other magical feats are by any, even of the wise, suspected; and by too many that would pass for wits derided and exploded' was shared by many. This scepticism extended to all the professionals necessarily involved in a prosecution – lawyers, clergy and doctors.

The historian of Scottish witchcraft, Christine Larner suggested that a necessary condition for witch-hunts was the combination of a peasant economy, a witch-believing peasantry and an active belief in the devil amongst educated people. She also suggested that witch-hunts continued while Christianity had a political importance (Larner, 1981, pp.193–4).

We have seen that the belief in the devil amongst educated people withered away. But what about the other factors?

What happened to witch-believing peasantries who were apparently using the persecution of witches as a relief for community tensions? Undoubtedly, sooth-saying and the use of charms, part of the older popular culture, survived, but were no longer subject to prosecution. The scepticism of all the professionals who were required to bring cases to court meant that the chance of getting anywhere with a case diminished rapidly. Yet belief in the supernatural and its power to do both good and harm did not just wither away in the face of the growing rationalism of the educated classes. Coward (p.496) suggests that there may have been little decline in the belief in witchcraft, while Briggs (p.211) suggests that fear of witches is still part of the rural mentality in France.

Rural life in all the countries we are concerned with was affected by the spread of an active clergy, whether it was covenanting ministers to the Highlands and Islands, priests inspired by Dominican missions in Brittany, or Nonconformist ministers to rural Yorkshire and Wales. As we saw in Unit 6, the opportunity for education was gradually being extended to more people, but the connection between the spread of education and the decline in witchcraft is difficult to establish.

Then there is the issue of women's authority. In Unit 9 I asked why it became such an issue in the late sixteenth and seventeenth centuries and ceased to be an issue by the eighteenth century. Evidence for England suggests that women's disputes which were serious enough to involve a third party and some kind of official intervention tended to turn into suits in the church courts about defamation. It may be that in England, reduced opportunities for women to work independently in the countryside diminished their authority as individuals. This was a product of changes in agricultural practices as regional specialization and an increase in sheep grazing and arable farming led to a reduction in the skilled work available to women and made them increasingly reliant on seasonal and unskilled work (see Coward, pp.470–3).

Larner suggested that the existence of a peasant economy was an important condition for a continuance in the belief in witchcraft. Clearly the development of capitalist agriculture in England coincided with the decline in witchcraft there. The gentry and yeomanry increased their land holding and the emergence of a class of landless labourers was a feature of the early eighteenth century. Perhaps the main impact on popular belief had to do with increasing geographical mobility which reduced the importance of individual grudges expressed as witchcraft accusations. As we have seen, people accused of witchcraft often had a long-standing reputation for their supposed powers. Where rural communities contained a relatively high proportion of recent immigrants, there was less opportunity for such long-standing reputations to develop. But many parts of France, western Ireland and the west and north of Scotland retained a peasant economy.

We lack a satisfactory explanation for the disappearance of witchcraft from the official record in the later seventeenth century. We have a partial explanation for its disappearance from the courts, but those historians who have concentrated on the rise of the witch-hunt might do well to turn their attention now to its disappearance. The extension of the power of the state has much to do with changes of attitudes. This was a period of considerable tension between state and church over their respective areas of authority. But it is also the period in which the power of the state ceases to need to be buttressed by theology. The concept of divine right disappears in the British Isles from 1688 and Louis XIV's pursuit of Catholic orthodoxy at home was undermined by his long-running dispute with the papacy. Perhaps we are brought back to Larner's point about the political importance of Christianity being a necessary condition for the existence of witchcraft beliefs, by what she calls elsewhere 'the eighteenth-century political dethronement of God' (Larner, 1981, p.14).

1685–1714

If 1685 marked the zenith of the power of the monarchies of France and England, what form did their power take over the following thirty years?

In the case of France, it is clear enough that after 1685 Louis could only expect to face a united alliance of European powers. He alienated his Protestant allies by the revocation of the Edict of Nantes and William of Orange's accession to the throne of England meant that England, formerly a capricious player in the formation of alliances against France because of Charles II's and James II's pro-French proclivities, was now permanently and centrally involved in anti-French alliances. England's growing commercial resources were now harnessed to the anti-French cause with the result that war might be extended beyond Europe to the colonies.

But the zenith of the French monarchy was not marked solely by events outside France. The years after 1685 saw a consolidation of the mechanisms of centralized royal power at home but also an erosion of the king's position by the demands of incessant warfare. Briggs suggests that during the final fifteen years of his life Louis XIV substantially lost control of the government, leaving it in the hands of his ministers and councils. But these ministers were not towering figures like Colbert, Le Tellier or Louvois. Most of the really great ministers and administrators were dead by the time the government moved to Versailles in 1682. There government departments became increasingly specialized and bureaucratic, though organized as they had been in the 1660s. Louis was better served in the later years of his reign by his generals, men such as Vauban and Vendôme, than he was by his ministers.

In England a more radical approach was taken, especially with the development of financial institutions. If 1685 marked the zenith of the power of the monarch alone, that of the monarch in parliament continued to expand in response to the demands of war. Professor J.R. Jones has written of England that:

> The rate of change in many areas of national life was perceptibly quickening in the years after 1688. There was not, as in the 1640s, a cataclysmic collapse of the established order, nor repetition of the drama of the world turned upside down by zealots and iconoclasts, but England after 1688 was entering the early stages of the processes of transformation that were to produce the first 'modern' society in Europe. (Jones, 1978, pp.358–9)

Historians and their evidence

In the course of your study you have encountered many different kinds of historical material. In this section of the unit I would like to evaluate how we use it and what kinds of conclusions we can draw from it. You might ask why have we left this exercise until now; shouldn't we have been doing this earlier in the course? In fact, we have already been doing something of this in the units, the *Anthology*, set books, Offprints, TV programmes, video, and audio, and in the TMAs. But you can see from what we have been doing that sources may be used in different ways, the same source may be used for different purposes. You'll remember that you looked at the Scottish Solemn League and Covenant of 1638 in both Units 3 and 7 for example. Let us first consider how historians present their material.

Secondary sources

Exercise   Think now about the secondary materials to which you have been introduced and consider:

1   what different types you have used;

2   what distinguishes them from materials produced in the seventeenth century.

Discussion   1   My list would go as follows:
   (a)   textbooks, books where the broad developments of the period are discussed without detailed reference to documents and original seventeenth-century material, but based upon a wide reading and knowledge of such sources. The set books and Mitchison's *Lordship to Patronage* (Offprint 8) are examples of such works. In addition to describing and analysing developments over the period they often discuss the debates which have taken place between historians. Coward, in particular, does this a good deal;
   (b)   historical surveys, books and articles based upon a similar wide range of material but engaging actively in historical debates. Examples of this are the pieces by Aylmer (Offprint 1), Russell (Offprint 7), and Bonney (Offprint 4);
   (c)   monographs (detailed studies of a particular period, subject or region making detailed reference to contemporary, that is to seventeenth-century, documents and publications). Such monographs might take the form of books, for example Sharon Kettering's *Patrons, Brokers and Clients*, or of articles, such as J.G. Simms's chapter on the war of the two kings (Offprint 15).

2   These works are produced by historians, reviewing the period and trying to answer questions on it in the light of their researches. The evidence of their research appears in the footnotes and references. Works such as these are produced with the explicit purpose of

analysing the events of the past. Materials produced in the seventeenth century may not have any such purpose, serving immediate needs, though sometimes including reflections upon larger subjects, such as in Mme de Maintenon's discussion of women's education. Many of the original materials which historians use are simply documents or artefacts created for an immediate and obvious reason. Such sources will tell us about the purpose for which they were created, but they may yield up other information, especially in conjunction with a variety of different materials.

Not only do historians produce different kinds of writing, they also use sources in different ways. They might disagree over the interpretation of documents, over the significance of an event or series of events, over the relative impact of different developments in precipitating change. You have seen something of this in the debates over the origins of the civil wars and in the discussion of what constitutes absolutism. The contemporary significance of historical debates may change. Karl S. Bottigheimer, reviewing writing on early modern Ireland published between 1982 and 1986, refers to two historians being 'not so much anti–nationalist as post nationalist in their views. With the modern Irish state securely established, it is no longer necessary to denounce every historical foreign intervention' (Bottigheimer, 1988, p.75). I write this in the autumn of 1994 following the IRA and Loyalist cease-fire which may lead to the evolution of another history of Ireland.

What is important to remember, is that historians are not simply trying to describe the passage of events, minute by minute, in the past. They are concerned with analysing evidence and using it to evaluate the extent of change. In order to do this, however, they need to have a thorough understanding of how their evidence came into being.

Primary sources

Most of the *Anthology* consists of seventeenth-century documents of the kind conventionally used by historians in writing about the seventeenth century. Many are reasonably straightforward, but some are rather more complicated.

Exercise Using the *Anthology* consider what kind of primary source the following items are:

1   the life of the Duke of Épernon (*Anthology*, I.10);

2   the Earl of Clarendon's *History of the Rebellion and Civil Wars in England* (*Anthology*, I. 20);

3   Bossuet's reflections on the Frondes (*Anthology*, I.19).

Discussion   All three works were composed some time after the period to which they actually refer. All three probably have some function beyond simply that of telling the story of the times, possibly some kind of explanatory or justificatory function.

1   The life of the duke was written soon after his death in 1642 by one of his secretaries. We might expect such a work to be favourable to the duke, if not adulatory.

2   Clarendon, an important actor in the events of the civil war in England, wrote his great history long after his political career had ended, when he was in exile abroad. We might expect, since he had to leave office in disgrace, that he would use the history to justify his actions. Note that it was not published until some years after his death.

3   Bossuet's reflections on the Frondes were made some thirty-five years later. He deliberately used the device of saying how terrible the Frondes were to enhance the significance of Louis XIV's 'miraculous reign'.

These are all documents produced in the seventeenth century but were written long after the events they describe. They are subject to the vagaries of memory, of the desire to set the record straight or to praise or exculpate people. Nevertheless, such documents are of great importance. We want to see what significance people accorded to their own times. Épernon's secretary was writing about him rather as biographers wrote about the Labour leader John Smith in the months after his death in 1994. Clarendon was writing about the civil war in much the same way that Churchill wrote about the Second World War. Bossuet was preaching about the Frondes rather as people speak about the D-Day landings on their anniversary.

Different kinds of historical source have different kinds of status and we form our ideas of developments in the past by consulting a wide variety of materials and constructing a composite picture. In Video 1 you saw how, by comparing buildings of similar function but evolving type, we could trace the development of changes in domestic life in a particular region, but that we needed other kinds of information to supplement our study of the buildings. We were not simply composing a snapshot, we were constructing an image of how living conditions had changed over the period. In the TV programmes we have tried, by comparing buildings over the longer period, to show how they reflect changes in people's lives. Now that you have reviewed the TV programmes, let us consider them in conjunction with the videos dealing with detailed aspects of those buildings.

Exercise   We have concentrated a good deal upon style, the style of individual buildings and the adaptation in the seventeenth century of older buildings. But what other aspects of buildings can inform our knowledge of life in the seventeenth century?

Discussion   We have considered the *setting* of buildings: in gardens, in relation to other buildings, to natural resources such as water, to communications, to urban spaces or to the landscape.

We have considered the *function* of buildings: in relation to political circumstances, to family structure, to livelihoods, to the local community or a wider community, to spiritual or ceremonial needs, to educational needs, to defensive needs.

We have considered the *use of space* within buildings in relation to their function, to ideas about public and private, to ideas about appropriate entrances and sequences of rooms.

(If you are in doubt about this, view TV2, TV3 and Video 8 for examples of buildings in different settings; TV4, TV8, Video 6 for examples of buildings with different functions; and Video 7, Video 10 and TV1 for examples of the different ways in which space might be used.)

Exercise   Consider what setting, function and use of space can tell us abut life in the seventeenth century.

Discussion   If you were to work through all the videos and TV programmes with these questions in mind, you would come up with a wealth of examples and this would be a useful revision exercise. I want to touch upon just a few to illustrate the kinds of thing you might mention.

Setting

We learn from the setting of buildings of the kinds of industrial activity (milling and linen processing) which might take place in the Breton countryside. Cloth was processed and sold in Chipping Camden, though it was no longer woven there by the seventeenth century.

The poor of the smaller urban centres were accommodated in almshouses near the centre of the town, not physically separated from the life of the town. The almshouses in Kinsale, in Youghal, in Stirling, in Chipping Camden and in Corsham were all close to the church, their position determined as much by the donor's desire to have his or her beneficence recognized as by the requirements of the inmates. Contrast this with the vast *hôpital*, set on the outskirts of Paris, away from the centre of the city. Was this to separate the citizens of Paris from medical and moral contagion by the inmates, or to protect inmates from the danger of further infection from the city?

Function

Industrial buildings tell us both about what industries were conducted, how the industry was organized and that the prospective profit was sufficient to justify capital expenditure on buildings. Buildings were usually only erected for livestock if the region was one of some insecurity, or if there was a profitable dairy industry. We have seen only a limited number of examples for a few regions, so it might be that there were specialized buildings for livestock in other parts of France where the economics of stock-rearing were different.

We learn from the houses of grandees that despite the use of modern styles of building, nobles retained the medieval notion that it was necessary to display power and status in extravagant houses and their ability to entertain lavishly. Wentworth explicitly tells us that he built Jigginstown to entertain the king in Ireland. This old-fashioned idea of hospitality persists, as we may see by the arrangements at Boughton House, although there is greater distinction between private and public spaces: a distinction which permeates other social groups as we may see in the newer buildings at Mézedern and Chipchase, at Plasnewydd, and in the alterations at Tronjoly.

Use of space

We can see from the palaces that monarchs deliberately used space: sequences of rooms to create a graduated approach to their presence. This was a highly hierarchical arrangement whereby those entering the monarch's presence might understand to what degree of intimacy they were admitted by the room in which they were received. At Versailles and Holyrood, for example, splendid sequences of rooms, each more magnificent that the last, led you towards the king. If you were one of his intimates you continued into smaller rooms, but they became more sumptuous.

In churches we can see how space was used to create a sense of awe before the altar, to draw attention to the most significant activity, whether it was preaching or the administration of sacraments, and to indicate the social standing of the living and the dead in the church.

There are many other connections and comparisons which you might make. Did you notice that lending money to the early Stuart kings, as George Heriot and Baptist Hicks did, helped the lenders to accumulate sufficient fortunes to engage in considerable charitable activities? Did you notice that building too great a mansion, as Wentworth and Fouquet did, might be the prelude to a spectacular disgrace for an ambitious royal servant? Did you notice how French kings relied almost entirely upon classical imagery to enhance their standing, while English monarchs used both classical and biblical imagery? Some of these connections are rather arbitrary, reflecting the nature of the places we chose to film, but they are always worth making and thinking about in order to try to think constructively about the forces at work in the past.

Understanding the past and how it evolves is necessarily dependent on the survival of evidence and this is not simply a random process. I'd like now to say a little about factors which have affected the survival of materials from the seventeenth century.

Survival and destruction of evidence

The chance survival of materials from past ages is always a consideration, but chance is mediated by all sorts of other factors which mean that there are many inbuilt biases in the materials which survive. Decay and destruction, both deliberate and accidental, take their toll of things which are now over 300 years old. Survival depends on all sorts of factors, though political stability certainly helps. Let us take some examples. The study of princes had been very much easier in this course because they caused written documents to be generated, they lived in durable houses, they inherited, bought and commissioned material objects which their descendants preserved both out of a sense of family piety and for their intrinsic value. Poorer people existed outside the world of the written word, lived in fragile buildings, moved about the place and had few possessions. As we saw in Unit 9, the poorest people who came into contact with the authorities left their mark because of the concern for record-keeping which increasingly distinguished seventeenth-century administration.

Figure 39
A depiction of a woman unusual for her fashion and learning. *Frontisiece of Jacques Du Bosc,* The Excellent Woman *described by her true characteristics and their opposites, translated by Theophilus Dorrington, 1692, London. Reproduced by permission of the Houghton Library, Harvard University.*

Thus, the world of the nobleman is more visible to us than the world of the gentleman, yeoman, artisan or peasant and the world of most women and children is less visible still. Governors and victors have left better records than the governed. We know more about the suppression of the Frondes than we know about the motives of rank-and-file participants, and about suppression of such revolts as that of the Nu-pieds and the Camisards than we know about the identities of the rebels. We have much better records for the parliamentary army in England in the 1640s than we have for the royalist army (for by the time that the royalists were able to account themselves the victors in 1660, eleven years had passed). We know more about the Protestants who were attacked by the Irish rebels in 1641 than we know about the leader of the rebels, Owen Roe O'Neill, and his motives or about the Confederation of Kilkenny. For periods of comparative peace we know even less about ordinary people's daily lives.

So inevitably written records are biased in favour of the literate, rich, powerful and male. But later developments have also caused some selective survivals. In France, much was lost during the French Revolution starting in 1789, especially records, buildings and artefacts connected with the church, the monarchy and the nobility. Coats of arms on buildings, for example, were often removed during this period. You can see where a coat of arms has been removed on the boss above the spiral staircase in the château of Tronjoly in Brittany shown in Video 5. There was damage to churches. The Sorbonne chapel shown in TV5 was turned into the Temple of Reason in 1794 and the Richelieu family tombs were removed. The royal palace of the Louvre became a museum in 1793 and was restored by Napoleon, but the château of Versailles had to wait until later in the nineteenth century to be restored by Louis Philippe, though its contents survived comparatively intact, having been taken to the Louvre. The revolutionary regimes were responsible for the foundation of many of the great archive collections upon which historians are so dependent, notably the National Archives established in 1789.

There is a good deal of debate about the extent of the destruction resulting from the English civil war. Recent work has suggested that much of the damage done to churches was the result of the iconoclasm of the Reformation during the 1530s and 1540s and that civil war destruction in churches was as often by civilians as by soldiers (Aston, 1988; Porter, 1994). However, Stephen Porter has also argued that the scale of military destruction was much greater than now appears because it was followed rapidly by rebuilding (Porter, 1994, p.133). Some buildings were partly demolished by government order following the end of the civil war so that they could not be used defensively again. The damage done to Nunney Castle in Somerset can still be seen, while Belvoir Castle in Leicestershire was replaced by a fine classical house commissioned in the 1650s by the Countess of Rutland.

The industrial revolution and the massive urban development of the nineteenth century changed the face of English towns, but the transformation of the countryside of England and Wales had begun in the eighteenth century with enclosure. The bombing of the Second World War destroyed much older building in London, a great toll was taken of the city livery companies and their records, for example. But it may fairly be said that town planners and the Department of Transport have probably been responsible for much more destruction or, which is as problematic for the historian, adaptation. The restoration of buildings is an extremely sensitive subject, one on which learned theses are written and acrimonious debates take place. It is becoming increasingly difficult to 'read' the history of buildings after their restoration or conversion. Even their preservation as museums, as we saw at Maison Cornec and Washington Old Hall, creates problems. Similarly, modern agricultural techniques have also much altered the landscape, though this had been under a continuous process of adaptation for some two hundred years.

Figure 40
Humble Scottish rural
dwellings of the
seventeenth century, *from
'The Prospect of the Abby of
Dunfermling', a plate in John
Slezer,* Theatrum Scotiae,
*1693. Reproduced by
permission of the British
Library Board.*

Such forces are also at work in Scotland, though perhaps not on quite such a large scale as in south-east England, because the pressure of population is slightly less. The Highland clearances of the late eighteenth and early nineteenth centuries were part of a larger process of change in which the population of the Scottish Highlands was removed to make way for sheep grazing, transforming both the landscape and rural economy of the region.

The history of Ireland in the seventeenth century is bedevilled by the absence of material evidence. Much of it probably never survived the seventeenth century. The buildings of the Gaelic Irish were taken over by English landlords and often demolished and replaced. At Pallas castle, co. Galway (TV4) the older buildings were simply abandoned and a new house was erected nearby in the eighteenth century. The newer house was destroyed during the twentieth century leaving only the older remains and the clear signs of an eighteenth-century park. In Ireland, as in all countries, towns were highly combustible. Attempts to get towns-people to build in stone and brick were thwarted by poverty and lack of materials.

The account of the destruction of many of Ireland's written records provides one of the rare occasions when a historian of the seventeenth century encounters the politics of the twentieth. The Deputy Keeper of the Public Records in Ireland recorded in his report that:

> On the night of Thursday, 13th April 1922, irregular military forces took possession of the Public Record Office as well as of the other offices of the Four Courts ... By the force of the explosion of the 30th June many documents of the various offices in the Four Courts, including the Public Record Office, were driven up into the air and came down in various parts of the City and suburbs, some

being picked up on the Hill of Howth. An appeal was made to people who were in possession of such documents to restore them to official custody ... A number of people brought in documents and fragments of documents, but very little of any importance or interest was recovered. (55th Report of the Deputy Keeper of the Public Records and Keeper of the State Papers in Ireland. Presented to both Houses of the Oireachatas, Dublin, Stationery Office, 1928, pp.3–4)

This episode echoes almost exactly the account of Colonel Michael Jones's capture of General Preston's papers at his victory at Dungan Hill. In a letter to parliament dated 29 September 1647, he wrote:

I gained them in a scattered way from several hands, as they were snatcht up in the field. (Trinity College Dublin MS 844, f.13)

This is not an attempt to provide a comprehensive list of civil and military strife which led to the survival or destruction of records of the past, whether written or otherwise, but I hope that it has indicated the kinds of issue we need to consider in observing that some records have survived and not others. These survivals have tended to favour the records of certain groups, but even when a large quantity of them remain, we still need to learn to interpret them. The records do not speak for themselves.

Reviewing the period

Let us now consider how different France and the British Isles were in 1714 from the way they were in 1620. You should start by working on the audio-cassette (AC2, section 8), in conjunction with the map at the beginning of this block and the map in the Illustration Book (Col. Pl. 3).

Having considered some of the changes which took place in the population over the period, let us return to Offprint 1. First read pp.5–6.

Exercise Which of the features of the state identified in Aylmer's article had changed in form in France and the British Isles over the period?

Discussion 1 The institutions of the state in France had become much more uniform over the period, regional differences and particular jurisdictions were increasingly replaced by a uniform system of government by royal officials. There were more of these officials then hitherto and there was also a large army.

In England and Wales institutions of the state remained substantially the same, though the ways in which they operated had altered. The powers of the monarchy were probably more limited and the powers of parliament more extensive than they were in 1620. I say probably because there is no doubt that William III used the war as a way of keeping control of aspects of government which might otherwise have come under parliament's control. Certainly the monarch had control of a very much larger army than he had had earlier in the period. Under the Act of Union, Scotland retained its own legal system but sent members of parliament to Westminster and it lost its own Privy Council. However, the government continued to rely upon nobles and their tenants to conduct administration in the more distant regions, though there was some attempt to involve the lairds, men of a slightly lower social level. In Ireland, the institutions remained much as they had been, but they were made effective and more coercive.

2   The French government had been moved from Paris to Versailles and, as we learnt from AC2, section 8, the bounds of its jurisdiction had altered substantially. In the British Isles, more government was centred upon London and London's will was more effective in the distant parts of the land.

3   If anything, it might be said that both states extended their monopolies of what Aylmer calls 'rule-making'. In France, independent jurisdictions and noblemen with substantial provincial power bases had made way for the government of the *intendants*. (Brittany, the last province to maintain some independence, received its *intendant* in 1689.) The independent privileges of the Huguenots had been eradicated. In England and Wales many feudal and customary jurisdictions had declined and the monarch in parliament enjoyed the monopoly of rule-making, though the monarch's capacity for independent rule-making was restricted. The effect of the abolition of the Scottish parliament is unclear, for its powers were not simply transferred to Westminster. Many aspects of Scottish local administration were conducted through the kirk sessions. In Ireland the last vestiges of Gaelic law and custom had disappeared, town corporations were entirely Protestant. For a time the Irish parliament (now entirely constituted of Protestant MPs) sought union with England, but Westminster expressed no interest. In the years after 1700 the Irish parliament seemed to have strengthened its position.

You may wish to work through the other features of the state as a revision exercise, making notes on the general categories a–d on pp.5–6 of Offprint 1, and then i–iii. You should use the indexes of the blocks and of the set books.

Now let us look at the way that the authors of the set books have summed up the period.

Exercise   Read Briggs, pp.206–11 and Coward, pp.493–7.

    1   What does each historian identify as the major transformation in the state?

    2   What reservations might we enter about these judgements?

Discussion   1   'From a Renaissance state very similar to her neighbours the country [France] developed into a distinctive 'absolute' monarchy which was widely admired and copied' (Briggs, p.206). But Briggs also emphasizes the rigidity of the state which had been constructed, able to do nothing but wage war and repress internal disorder.

Coward is reluctant to commit himself on the subject of constitutional change, but having said the 'royal court remained the centre of politics' (p.496), he goes on to say that 'Both the royal government and parliament emerged in 1714 with enhanced powers' (p.467). A very important point is being made here. It is royal government *and* parliament. Without parliament the monarch had retained great personal power, but he, she or they could not conduct government without it in the way that Charles I had been able to do in the 1630s. The scope of control over the state was extended by the crown and parliament working together.

2 Notice that Briggs is assessing the period from 1560 to 1715, so his judgements are based upon changes which had taken place before 1620. It is possible to argue that by 1620 France was no longer a Renaissance state. Notice, too, that the shadow of the French Revolution is cast over this summing up: 'on most fronts the potential for further change was artificially restricted' (p.206). The passage beginning 'However confused, impractical, or reactionary' travels from the French Revolution to the Gaullist France of the 1950s and 1960s.

Coward starts his book in 1603, a mere 17 years before we begin. He is concerned with the extent to which the study of change obscures continuities in society and with the distorting effect of looking for the origins of modern developments, in particular for the roots of Britain's later industrial and commercial success. He is so concerned to warn us about the dangers of distortion that he does perhaps diminish the extent of such changes as took place. Certainly English society in 1714 was not a 'modern' society, but it was very unlike the England of 1620.

That this is a period of continuing interest to historians is evidenced by the differences between the first edition of Coward, published in 1980, and the second published in 1994. In the first he wrote: 'Like many other European states ... [in the 1680s] England seemed set to become an absolutist state' (Coward, 1980, p.291). In the same section, the introduction to chapter 11, in the second edition he writes 'England seemed set to follow the trend of other European states ... towards strong, centralized, authoritarian government' (Coward, 1994, p.333). He has also added a footnote about the meaning of the term 'absolutism'. This is a good example of how a combination of reflection and new research may cause a historian to revise an earlier assessment.

To show that other historians too differ from Briggs and Coward, here is a selection of comments by historians of very different views.

[Late seventeenth-century England] is a world in which governments put first the promotion of production, for policy is no longer determined by aristocrats whose main economic activity is consumption … The men of property are secure and unfettered in their control of local government: as taxpayers they determine government policy. (Hill, 1980, p.263)

At the death of Louis XIV in 1715, the internal situation in France offered little evidence of the strong and glorious spectacle by which Europe characterised the reign of that great monarch, whom many nations hated but all respected and feared. (Mettam, 1977, p.266)

Discounting the libertarian rhetoric which 1688–9 generated on the part of a small but vocal minority, it is possible to see that the effective powers of the [English] Crown continued to grow. (Clark, 1986, p.89)

The financial and tax system of seventeenth-century France was as much a compromise as its political system. Those compromises were a symbol of the king's weakness, as well as the source of his real power. (Collins, 1988, pp.221–2)

In England the lesson of 1688, enshrined in what were known as Revolution principles, was that government must take into account (and be sensitive to changes in) the interests of the nation. (Jones, 1978, p.360)

These perhaps contradictory observations suggest that whilst there appear to be divergent outcomes of the period 1620–1714, there are also very great similarities. Neither absolute nor limited monarchy came about overnight, but as the consequence of a long period of political, social and religious upheaval. In both states the process of discarding a medieval society based upon a system of feudal ties of obligation between different strata is seen as the process of creating a modern state with its attendant political and economic machinery. John Morrill suggests that the achievements of French absolutism were that:

> In the course of the seventeenth century the monarchy extinguished all other patrimonies and ancient principalities within the bounds of the kingdom. Louis XIII and XIV ruled as kings of France, not as king here, duke there. Their writs, the same writs, ran everywhere. The Crown enunciated the doctrine 'no land without seigneur'… The seventeenth century witnessed the creation of a common coinage throughout France and the sponsorship of linguistic unity and purity. The Crown's legislative autonomy was acknowledged (in the sense of the making of law: total success would have involved the codification and reissuing under royal authority of all customary law and this was not achieved). The king asserted (though this was periodically challenged) complete freedom to choose his own ministers, advisers, judges, a freedom restricted in practice but not in theory by the spread of venality and the introduction of the *paulette*. The king's claim to be the source of all justice was greatly strengthened. His ability to tax at will, or at least within the limits of practical prudence, his ability to sustain a large standing army (and, as the century wore on, to monopolise coercive power) and his growing control of the Church in France, most obviously through the restoration of religious unity through

the revocation of the edict of Nantes, more subtly through his rights within the Church, and sponsorship of the catholic reformation, are all extensions of inherent strengths of the monarchy. (Morrill, 1978, pp.962–3)

But aren't some of these achievements familiar from the other side of the Channel? The monarch ruled the British Isles as monarch, and indeed had done so since 1603. Seigneurial jurisdictions, in England largely attached to manorial lordships, were diminishing in importance. The abolition of feudal dues which had taken place during the civil war was confirmed at the Restoration. The king's writ ran everywhere, though it was a different writ in Scotland and Ireland from that in England. The monarch had a free hand to appoint ministers, attempts by parliament to interfere in this right were generally unsuccessful, and judges' appointments were personal to the monarch. The crown's powers to raise more revenue increased, as can be seen by the much higher levels of taxation of the later seventeenth century, but its ability to do so without parliament was reduced. The monarch's power to keep a standing army actually increased during the period. The standing army controversy of 1697–9 (see Coward pp.385–6) appears to have been a humiliating defeat for William III, but he had far greater power over the military than had Charles I.

But apart from these similarities, there are some important differences. There wasn't a common coinage throughout the British Isles. The crown's legislative autonomy was probably diminished by the greater role of parliament, though considerable powers were retained. Where British monarchs had more extensive powers than their French counterparts was in the appointment of royal officials, since the sale of offices was insignificant and few offices were hereditary. On the other hand, the number of crown officers was minuscule by comparison with France, given that most provincial officers were part time and amateur. Another marked difference was the way in which control over the church was exercised. One of the most important aspects of the Glorious Revolution was the Toleration Act of 1689 which established religious pluralism as a principle in England and Wales. As we have seen, religious matters were rather differently dealt with in Scotland and Ireland. In Scotland crown control over the church was much diminished by the abolition of episcopacy, though crown appointments remained an important element in the Churches of England and Ireland.

I have left until last the issue of cultural homogenization and linguistic purity. It is sometimes asserted that a process of cultural homogenization took place in the British Isles in the early modern period. Certainly, for men in the political nation the use of the English language was essential and it is likely that more people in the non-English-speaking parts of the British Isles became bi-lingual in this period. The use of Latin and legal French was declining. It had been state policy in the sixteenth century to extirpate the Irish language as part of the attempt to de-Gaelicize the country in the interests of English supremacy. Later, under Queen Elizabeth and in the seventeenth century there developed an interest in the Irish language. The queen encouraged her officials in Ireland to use Irish and she provided the press and the type to produce an Irish translation of the Bible. The New Testament appeared in 1603 and the type was used to print a Protestant catechism and other works. Irish was regarded as essential for proselytizing and in the later years of the seventeenth century, the language was being taught to divinity students at Trinity College, Dublin with the approval of the successive provosts Narcissus Marsh and Robert Huntingdon. Nevertheless, many Protestant ministers did not speak Irish and regarded its use as retrograde, especially because it was strongly associated with the activities of the Catholic clergy, educated on the continent and returning to Ireland to spread the word. Written English in Ireland increasingly conformed to English usage, but spoken English seems to have been greatly influenced by Irish, especially in regions where there was little contact with English speakers from England. We have seen in Unit 6 something of the attempt to eradicate the use of the Gaelic language in Scotland (often referred to as 'Irish' in the seventeenth century). The use of the Welsh language did not diminish, because of the translation of the Scriptures and the Circulating Schools, though bilingualism probably became commoner amongst the gentry in search of political advancement.

The declining use of these languages was not simply the result of circumstances which forced more people to use the English language, it was also to do with cultural changes which meant that fewer people were, for example, writing poetry in the bardic tradition. Yet in Scotland there was a flowering of poetry in Gallic written by women, a development not replicated in other Gaelic regions. The process by which the numbers of people using these languages declined seems to have amounted to more than straightforward English cultural imperialism, but there has been little comparative research on this subject.

Finally, taking the longer view can we say that the upheavals of the mid-seventeenth century substantially contributed to the changes which took place in the later seventeenth century? This is a tricky question to consider because inevitably it raises complicated issues of causality. You might wish to argue that the upheavals were the result of longer-term structural changes and that it was these changes which wrought the real revolution. Undoubtedly the English civil war was a tremendously important event in the history of England and Wales. It is not clear whether the war in Scotland really marked a turning point in Scottish history rather than in the relations between England and Scotland, and the same might be said of Ireland. It was as much because of the upheavals in England as in Ireland that the massive land transfer took place in Ireland. In France, without the Frondes there would not have been the same general assent to the idea of order as an absolute good, which legitimated Louis XIV's reign; this takes us back to where this unit began.

I am tempted to wish you good luck with the exam, and perhaps there is an element of fortune in which subjects you have revised and which subjects we have set questions on. If, however, you have worked through the course material thoroughly, done the TMAs and studied the specimen exam and its guidance notes carefully, you should not have much difficulty. Just keep calm and answer the questions as accurately as possible. But good luck all the same.

References

Aston, M. (1988), *England's Iconoclasts I,* Oxford University Press, Oxford.

Bottigheimer, K. S. (1988), 'The new new Irish history', *Journal of British Studies,* 27, p.78 ff.

Burke, P. (1992), *The Fabrication of Louis XIV,* Yale University Press, New Haven.

Campbell, P.R. (1993), *Louis XIV,* Seminar Studies in History, Longman, Harlow.

Collins, J. B. (1988), *The Fiscal Limits of Absolutism: Direct Taxation in Early Seventeenth-Century France,* University of California Press, Berkeley.

Clark, J. C. D. (1986), *Revolution and Rebellion: State and Society in England in the Seventeenth and Eighteenth Centuries,* Cambridge University Press, Cambridge.

Déon, M. (1991), *Louis XIV par lui-même,* éditions Gallimard, Paris.

Ford, F. L. (1965), *Robe and Sword: the Regrouping of the French Aristocracy after Louis XIV,* Harper Paperback, New York.

Goubert, P. (1970), *Louis XIV and Twenty Million Frenchmen,* Allen Lane, London, translated by Anne Carter. (First published by Fayard, Paris, 1966.)

Hill, C. (1980), *The Century of Revolution 1603–1714,* Nelson, Walton on Thames.

Holmes, G. (1967), *British Politics in the Age of Anne,* Macmillan, London.

Hughes, A. (1987), *Politics, Society and Civil War in Warwickshire 1620–1660,* Cambridge University Press, Cambridge.

Jones, J. R. (1978), *Country and Court: England 1658–1714,* Edward Arnold, London.

Larner, C. (1981), *Enemies of God: the Witch-hunt in Scotland,* Chatto and Windus, London.

Mettam, R. (1977), *Government and Society in Louis XIV's France,* Macmillan, London.

Miller, J. (1987), *Bourbon and Stuart: Kings and Kingship in France and England in the Seventeenth Century,* George Philip, London.

Morrill, J. (1978), 'French absolutism as limited monarchy', *Historical Journal,* 21.

Myers, W. (1986), *Restoration and Revolution,* Croom Helm, Beckenham.

Parker, D. (1983), *The Making of French Absolutism,* Edward Arnold, London.

Porter, S. (1994), *Destruction in the English Civil Wars,* Alan Sutton, Stroud.

Simms, J. G. (1986), 'The establishment of Protestant ascendancy, 1691–1714', in T. W. Moody and W. E. Vaughan (eds), *Eighteenth Century Ireland 1691–1800,* vol. IV of *A New History of Ireland,* Clarendon Press, Oxford.

Thomas, K. V. (1973), *Religion and the Decline of Magic,* Penguin, Harmondsworth.

Index